# inspiring
## THE BEST IN STUDENTS

# inspiring
## THE BEST IN STUDENTS

**JONATHAN C. ERWIN**

 Alexandria, Virginia

**ASCD®**

1703 N. Beauregard St. • Alexandria, VA 22311-1714 USA
Phone: 800-933-2723 or 703-578-9600 • Fax: 703-575-5400
Web site: www.ascd.org • E-mail: member@ascd.org
Author guidelines: www.ascd.org/write

Gene R. Carter, *Executive Director;* Nancy Modrak, *Publisher;* Scott Willis, *Director, Book Acquisitions & Development;* Julie Houtz, *Director, Book Editing & Production;* Ernesto Yermoli, *Editor;* Sima Nasr, *Senior Graphic Designer;* Mike Kalyan, *Production Manager;* Marlene Hochberg, *Typesetter*

All Web links in this book are correct as of the publication date above but may have become inactive or otherwise modified since that time. If you notice a deactivated or changed link, please e-mail books@ascd.org with the words "Link Update" in the subject line. In your message, please specify the Web link, the book title, and the page number on which the link appears.

PAPERBACK ISBN: 978-1-4166-0979-7          ASCD product #110006   n5/10
Also available as an e-book (see Books in Print for the ISBNs).

Quantity discounts for the paperback edition only: 10–49 copies, 10%; 50+ copies, 15%; for 1,000 or more copies, call 800-933-2723, ext. 5634, or 703-575-5634. For desk copies: member@ascd.org.

**Library of Congress Cataloging-in-Publication Data**

Erwin, Jonathan C., 1954-
  Inspiring the best in students / Jonathan C. Erwin.
    p. cm.
  Includes bibliographical references and index.
  ISBN 978-1-4166-0979-7 (pbk. : alk. paper)  1. Motivation in education.  I. Title.
  LB1065.E79 2010
  370.15′4—dc22
                                        2009053849

20 19 18 17 16 15 14 13 12 11 10       1 2 3 4 5 6 7 8 9 10 11 12

*This book is dedicated to my beautiful wife, Holly,*
*who inspires the best in me.*

# inspiring
## THE BEST IN STUDENTS

# ACKNOWLEDGMENTS

Writing a book is a risky prospect. In order to sustain the time and effort involved, the writer needs to have confidence that the final product will not only be published, but also read—in the case of this book, in a way that will positively impact students' lives. My confidence in this book has been sustained significantly by the school leaders, teachers, and students I have had the privilege to work with during my career, including Turi Nilson and Erika Brockman, the courageous founders and leaders of the Southwest Baltimore Charter School, and their teachers and staff; Heidi Greene, Trish Hermance, and the faculty of the Campus Community School in Dover, Delaware; Tamara Larson, Peggy Beach, and the staff of the Lewiston-Porter Intermediate and Primary Schools in Youngstown, New York; Lockport City School District leaders Terry Carbone, Shelley Bradley, and Marianne Curry-Hall, and the staff of Roy B. Kelley Elementary; and Diane Vance, the director of Smart Character Choices, as well as the school leaders, faculty members, and wonderful students of the Smart Character Choices schools in Michigan—the Chatfield School in Lapeer, Creative Technologies Academy in Cedar Springs, the Dearborn Academy in Dearborn, and Randels Elementary in Flint. The aforementioned educators have applied many of the ideas presented in this book in their schools and classrooms with positive social, emotional, and academic results for their students.

*Inspiring the Best in Students* would not have been possible without Dr. William Glasser, whose "choice theory" provides much of the foundation for this book. In addition to Dr. Glasser, I want to thank the following leaders and faculty of the William Glasser Institute who have helped me to understand

and apply the ideas of internal control psychology (and, in so doing, have become good friends): Bob Sullo, Al Katz, Linda Harshman, Peter Appel, Sue Tomaszewski, Kathy Curtiss, Bruce Allen, and Lynn Sumida.

Also, I am grateful to the publishing staff at ASCD for their dedication to producing high-quality books for educators worldwide. I would particularly like to thank Scott Willis, for his encouragement and confidence in my work, and Ernesto Yermoli, whose editing skills and understanding of internal control psychology have made this a tighter, more readable book.

Finally, I want to thank my wife, Holly, and my three children, Nate, Liam, and Laena, for inspiring me and encouraging me through every step of the writing process.

# INTRODUCTION

*Inspiring the Best in Students* was born out of my 23 years working with children and adolescents, first as an English teacher, drama director, and coach; next as a staff development specialist; and finally as an education consultant, often invited to work with schools' most challenging students. I entered the classroom in 1986, well prepared to teach English, but not nearly as well prepared to teach kids. My preparation focused more on teaching content than on understanding how to connect with, motivate, and manage adolescents. Most of my education courses were theoretical survey classes, with little exposure to real children until student teaching, which was during my last semester. Needless to say, there was a lot of "on-the-job training."

During my first few years of teaching, I gradually started to understand the fascinating challenges that adolescents present: their drive to challenge, critique, and eventually separate from the adults in their life; their constant testing of the limits imposed on them; their lack of impulse control; and the ongoing drama involving relationships with their peers. Then one summer, I took an intensive course in what is now known as choice theory (Glasser, 1998). For me, as for many of the teachers I've worked with over the years, choice theory articulates a philosophy of teaching that resonated, one based on positive relationships and inspiration instead of power and control.

I first applied choice theory to my classroom by using the ideas to create a needs-satisfying learning environment, characterized by positive relationships, student voice and choice, and differentiated, engaging teaching and learning strategies. I explain this process in detail in my first book, *The Classroom of*

*Choice: Giving Students What They Need and Getting What You Want* (Erwin, 2004). As I continued my work toward certification in choice theory, I decided to try an approach to literature that involved students in analyzing literary characters' actions, thoughts, and motivation through a choice theory lens.

To do this, I needed to teach my students some choice theory. When I did, I felt like I'd struck gold. My students learned the concepts easily and eagerly, and they applied them in ways that yielded a deeper understanding of literary characters, conflicts, and themes. Serendipitously, students gained insight not only into literary characters but into themselves and others. Choice theory provided us with a common language and understanding for meaningful class discussions and problem solving, as well as a plethora of writing, speaking, and listening activities and assignments. It also improved relationships between myself and my students, as well as among my students. Although I didn't know it at the time, this was my first experience with a kind of character education called social-emotional learning (SEL). I was hooked.

I continued to teach choice theory, augmenting it with other, related SEL and character strategies. Behavior problems all but disappeared, students enjoyed each other and liked coming to class, and students' report card grades and standardized test scores (in New York state, it was the Regents ELA exam) continued to improve. By this time I was teaching 11th and 12th grade students. When graduates returned after their first semester or year in college, or when on leave from the military, they mentioned SEL as benefiting them at least as often as the writing skills they had acquired.

In fact, one August afternoon, I received a call from one of my seniors who'd graduated a little over a year before. His name was Mike. He was a bright, funny kid, the kind who make you glad they are never absent. He was a sensitive student from a tough home environment, and I worried about him. During his last semester of high school, he was using marijuana (probably other drugs as well) and was in a destructive relationship with a troubled girl. On the eve of graduation, he had no plans other than to try to find a job out of state and live with his girlfriend. When he called that day, the conversation was short, but he let me know that he had moved to Florida to live with his mother and stepdad, had broken up with his girlfriend, had completed an intensive outpatient drug rehabilitation program, and was planning to enroll in a community college. "I just wanted to say thanks. My life's a lot better now," he concluded, "and it's because of that choice stuff you used to teach us."

"I'm glad that helped you, Mike, but if you think it was the 'choice stuff' that did it, then I'm going to have to lower your grade," I kidded.

He thought for a second. "Yeah, yeah. I know, I know—it was me."

I wished him luck, said good-bye, hung up, and basked in one of those validating moments that come along every once in a while in education. As I thought about Mike and the difficult life choices he'd made recently, I knew that he would have gotten an *A* in my English class with or without the SEL. But without it, that phone call would never have come, and Mike's life may have been terribly different. In Chapter 1, you will find that there is a solid research-based rationale for character education and SEL, and although educational practice must be informed by good scholarly research, it is stories like Mike's and others I'll share throughout the book that prove to me the importance of integrating social-emotional learning and character development into the curriculum.

## The Intended Audience

This book is intended for anyone who works with young people and wants to help them develop the intra- and interpersonal skills required to be a successful, contributing member of society. It was originally intended for teachers of grades 3–12. Most of the student-centered activities are designed with those ages in mind, but many could be simplified for younger children or made more complex for young adults. Using the concepts explained in this book, primary school teachers also should find it easy to create activities and teaching strategies of their own. Additionally, this book could be a useful resource for school counselors, social workers, coaches, members of the clergy, community youth organizations, parents, and any others who want to promote positive youth development.

## How to Use This Book

This book can be used in as many ways as there are schools or classrooms. Here are a few general ideas.

Ideally, schools would use this book as a foundational resource for broadening the scope of their mission, to include educating the whole child through the integration of social-emotional learning into the curriculum, thus promoting strong character. To do this, teachers might follow the book chapter by chapter as each new concept builds on the last, choosing activities that are developmentally appropriate. Integrating this book's content with the general curriculum, schools would probably need two full years to teach the entire book.

Another approach might be to divide the book's curriculum by grade level: grade 3, learning the knowledge and skills in Chapters 1 and 2; grade 4, Chapters 3 and 4; and so forth. In elementary schools, the *Inspiring the Best* curriculum might be taught in special blocks of time to two or three classes at once by a school counselor, teacher, or team of teachers who have a special interest in character development. Or it might be more invisibly integrated into daily lessons by the general education teacher.

In secondary schools, this curriculum might fall into the domain of the school counselor or the English, social studies, or health teachers, as much of the content can be very easily integrated into those curricula. Many schools have instituted an advisory period for students to develop a mentoring relationship with a teacher (some use homeroom this way). I know from visiting hundreds of schools that those advisories can be either highly effective or a waste of everyone's time, depending on how they are structured. *Inspiring the Best in Students* provides a ready-made curriculum and dozens of student-friendly activities that would build student-teacher relationships while teaching useful information and skills.

Another way of using this book is as a kind of grab bag of information and activities that target specific student needs. For example, you might address impulse control or teach students the social skill of active listening. Some of the activities—the Inside-Outside Circle or the class meeting, for example—might be adapted to teach not only character and social-emotional learning, but also the academic curriculum. Although using the activities out of context may not be as effective as if they were part of a coherent character development program, they would still encourage students' social and emotional development. Any way you choose to use this book, I thank you for doing whatever you can to inspire the best in kids.

# 1 | INSPIRING THE BEST

If you are reading this book, you almost certainly work with young people. Maybe you are a teacher, counselor, or school administrator. Or maybe you are a social worker, therapist, mentor, coach, or youth development leader. In whatever capacity you work with children or teenagers, you want to inspire what is best in them. If you are reading this book, you also probably have experienced a respectable amount of personal success in your life. Before considering what is involved in bringing out the best in students, I ask you to reflect on the personal traits or qualities that have enabled you to experience success.

These personal traits are likely to include, among others, responsibility, respect, perseverance, honesty, integrity, patience, a strong work ethic, self-discipline, optimism, empathy, compassion, and cooperation. We need these characteristics to survive and thrive in a complex, competitive world. Of course, it is virtually impossible to demonstrate all of these qualities consistently; however, without exhibiting them at important life junctures, you would not have experienced the degree of success that you have. And without the positive relationships and achievements that your character traits have made possible, you probably would not experience the degree of happiness you enjoy in life.

Today's students face an even more challenging world than we did. Therefore, it is more important than ever for young people to develop the qualities that enabled our success, character traits that will help them learn and achieve well in school, perform satisfactorily in the workplace, communicate effectively, and develop and maintain positive, trusting relationships in their lives.

This book, then, is about promoting character development. This first chapter will address fundamental questions about the prospect of integrating a character education initiative into what many perceive as an already overwhelming curriculum. Subsequent chapters will focus on specific information and skills that support students' character development and will provide engaging, research-based teaching strategies.

## The Need for Character Education or Social-Emotional Learning (SEL)

Disturbing statistics suggest that what we are currently doing in schools to help students meet the challenges of contemporary society leaves many children and adolescents behind. In fact, 20 to 60 percent of urban, suburban, and rural high school students become chronically disengaged from school—not counting those who already dropped out (Klem & Connell, 2004). In America's 10 largest cities, the high school graduation rates hover around 50 percent. In New York City, Baltimore, and Detroit, graduation rates in 2006 were a dismal 38.9 percent, 38.5 percent, and 21.7 percent, respectively (Toppo, 2006). Furthermore, approximately 30 percent of high school students "participate in or experience multiple high-risk behaviors (e.g., substance abuse, sex, violence, depression, attempted suicide) that interfere with school performance and jeopardize their potential for life success" (Payton et al., 2008, p. 3).

Unfortunately, for at least the last decade, the emphasis—or, some might argue, the obsession—in U.S. education has been on raising academic standards and student (and teacher) accountability through frequent standardized testing. I'm not arguing that we should lower academic standards, nor should we decrease accountability. However, as a society, we need to address the questions, What is the purpose of public education? Is it enough to focus on students' academic and intellectual competence alone and leave all other aspects of their development to chance? The statistics shared here shout, "No!" If we are to help all children reach their full potential; become contributing, successful members of a democratic society; and improve the unsettling trends just discussed, we must address the development and education of the whole child.

What, then, are the dimensions of a whole human being? First is the physical dimension: a person's health, strength, motor skills, and athletic ability. Next is the intellectual dimension: memory, learning, thinking skills, problem solving, and creativity. The third dimension covers emotions: emotional awareness and understanding, self-regulation, self-motivation, and self-esteem. The fourth dimension is the social dimension: forming and maintaining positive interactions with family, friends, peers, coworkers, the community, and society at large. Finally, there is the spiritual dimension: our relationship with something larger than ourselves, whether we call it God, Allah, Jehovah, a Higher Power, Nature, Humanity, or even our purpose or legacy.

The human dimension with which schools are primarily concerned is that of the intellect. In response to pressure from federal and state education departments to raise academic standards and increase accountability, schools emphasize intellectual development, particularly in math and verbal areas, almost to the exclusion of everything else. As educators, we fail our students if we don't also address two other important human dimensions: the social and emotional. By intentionally helping students develop those facets of themselves, we will simultaneously improve both their physical and intellectual development.

Today, there is an increased call to promote the education of the whole child. Stating that educating "the whole child cannot happen if emphasis is placed solely on academic achievement" (p. 11), *ASCD's Learning Compact Redefined: A Report of the Commission on the Whole Child* (2007) recommends that school districts incorporate social and emotional learning (SEL) into their programs. Over the last dozen years in my role as a consultant, I have often been invited to work with students who have been expelled from their home schools or who have been involved with the judicial system. I am frequently struck by how intellectually bright and creative these students are. Their problems don't stem from the inability to succeed academically. In almost every case, it is the social and emotional knowledge and skills that have been deficient, which often leads to academic failure and chronically disruptive or antisocial behavior. If we fail to address these needs, we are indirectly sentencing many of these students to a lifetime of problems and burdening society with all the emotional, social, and fiscal issues that accompany them.

There is another important consideration. Just as a developmental window of opportunity exists for more easily acquiring a second language, the time when the frontal cortex gradually matures (the elementary, middle, and high school years) is the optimal time to encourage emotional, social, and moral development. "By leaving the emotional lessons children learn to chance," writes Goleman (1995), "we risk largely wasting the window of opportunity presented by the slow maturation of the brain to help children cultivate a healthy [social and] emotional repertoire" (p. 286). Ideally, social and emotional skills are taught from early childhood through early adulthood, but as we now know, the brain isn't completely developed until the early to mid-20s (Jensen, 2006), and even fully mature adults are able to grow new neurons. Neither intellectual IQ nor social or emotional IQ is set at birth or in childhood. So although childhood and adolescence are the optimal times to nurture SEL, it is never too late to do so and should not be simply left to chance.

## What Is SEL?

Jonathan Cohen (1999), the director of the Center for Social and Emotional Education (CSEE), explains that SEL is the development of "the skills and attitudes necessary to acquire social and emotional competencies" (p. 12). Daniel Goleman (1995), author of *Emotional Intelligence*, defines emotional competency as having the knowledge and skills that channel "behaviors toward a positive end . . . whether it be in controlling impulse and putting off gratification, regulating our moods [and emotions] so they facilitate rather than impede thinking, motivating ourselves to persist and try, try again in the face of setbacks, or finding ways to . . . perform more effectively" (p. 95). Yet, emotional intelligence cannot be isolated from social intelligence; almost all emotions have a social component: "You can't separate the cause of an emotion from the world of relationships—our social interactions are what drive our emotions" (Goleman, 2006, p. 83). Social competency, then, involves our ability to navigate the world of human relationships, whereas emotional competency enables us to cope with the myriad emotions that relationships involve—and to do so with positive results.

The Collaborative for Academic, Social, and Emotional Learning (CASEL) defines social and emotional learning as the process through which children and adults acquire the knowledge, attitudes, and skills to

- Recognize and manage their emotions
- Set and achieve positive goals
- Demonstrate caring and concern for others
- Make responsible decisions
- Handle interpersonal situations effectively. (Payton et al., 2008, p. 4)

Simply stated, emotional learning is gaining the knowledge, the desire, and ability to use *intra*personal skills, whereas social learning is gaining the knowledge, the desire, and the ability to use *inter*personal skills. In terms of character development, social and emotional learning enables and inspires character traits such as respect for self and others, personal and social responsibility, optimism, a strong work ethic, perseverance, compassion, cooperation, and honesty.

## What Research Says About SEL

More than ever before, educators are research driven. Fortunately, the latest research involving SEL (and character development in general) is compelling, positively affecting everything from students' individual health and wellness to significant increases in standardized test scores.

In *Smart & Good High Schools*, Lickona and Davidson (2005) report on their studies of the impact of character education in general on schools:

At every developmental level—elementary, middle, and high school— students who experienced quality character education programs outperformed comparison groups not only on measures of social behavior but also on measures of academic learning. There's an emerging body of hard evidence that we'll get an academic payoff when we invest in developing character as the foundation for excellence. (p. 211)

Indeed, since Lickona and Davidson's report, a hard body of evidence has continued to emerge. Most recently, a long-awaited report, the biggest study of its kind ever done, demonstrates the significant positive impact SEL can have on students and schools. Entitled *The Positive Impact of Social and Emotional Learning for Kindergarten to Eighth-Grade Students* (Payton et al., 2008), it "summarizes results from three large-scale reviews of the impact of social and emotional learning programs on elementary and middle-school students" (p. 3). The three reviews included 317 studies involving 324,303 children. Students in effective SEL programs demonstrated improvement in multiple areas of their personal, social, and academic lives, including these:

- Social-emotional skills
- Attitudes toward self, school, and others
- Social behaviors
- Conduct problems
- Emotional distress (anger, anxiety, and depression)

Notably, SEL programming "yielded an average gain on achievement test scores of 11 to 17 percentile points" (p. 6). Moreover, SEL programs and interventions were beneficial across grades K–8; for schools in rural, suburban, and urban settings; and with racially and ethnically diverse student populations. The authors of the report compared the findings in their review with findings obtained in reviews of evidence-based interventions conducted by other researchers and concluded that "SEL programs are among the most successful interventions ever offered to school-aged youth" (p. 6).

While CASEL's report focuses on K–8 SEL programs, a growing body of research supports the *Good & Smart High Schools* report, suggesting that high school is not too late to introduce character education. My own personal experience bears this out. One of my first experiences teaching character through SEL involved working with an alternative high school near Elmira, New York. Linda Hillman, the principal at the time, was interested in her students' learning choice theory and the social and emotional skills that went along with it. Over the course of the 1999–2000 school year, I worked with the entire student body in groups of 10 to 15 for three full days (with two or three teachers and paraprofessionals participating as well). By March 1, 2000, the referral rate had decreased 78 percent. With continued work with new students, and with teachers reviewing and supporting the previous learning, the rate decreased another 13 percent the next year. We had made a significant impact on the school culture and climate.

## The Characteristics of an Effective SEL or Character Program

The powerful findings discussed here were all based on effective character education or SEL programs. It is important to understand what research says about the common elements of programs that are deemed effective. In 2005, the Character Education Partnership (CEP), along with the John Templeton Foundation, funded research to "derive practical conclusions about character education implementation from the existing literature" (p. 2). Authors Berkowitz and Bier "selected programs with well-designed research"; investigated what the research revealed about the effectiveness of the programs; and after considering 78 studies, "identified 33 programs with scientific evidence supporting their effectiveness in promoting character development in students" (p. 7).

The authors then looked at the strategies those effective programs had in common. In their report, entitled *What Works in Character Education: A Research-Driven Guide for Educators*, they state that programs that have demonstrated a positive effect include the following elements:

- Professional development for teachers
- Peer interaction
- Direct teaching
- Skill training and practice
- An explicit agenda
- Family or community involvement
- Models and mentors
- Integration into the academic curriculum
- A multistrategy approach

Similarly, the CASEL report cited earlier analyzed successful SEL initiatives and found that they shared the following attributes:

- They were *sequenced*—applying a planned set of activities to develop knowledge and skills in a step-by-step fashion;
- They were *active*—using engaging forms of learning, including role-play and behavioral rehearsal;
- They were *focused*—devoting sufficient time exclusively to developing social and emotional skills; and
- They were *explicit*—targeting specific social and emotional information and skills.

In addition to these criteria, research supports the use of an intrinsic-oriented approach to teaching in general, whether it be character development, SEL, or academic subjects. Many character education models use an extrinsic-oriented approach, with "caught you being good" tickets and various rewards for demonstrating positive social or emotional (or character) behavior. Although recognition and positive, specific teacher feedback are important to student motivation (Marzano, Pickering, & Pollock, 2001), the use of tangible rewards tends to backfire (Ryan & Deci, 2002).

Instead of expending energy on reward systems that don't work and often distract teachers and students alike from the ultimate goal, it would be far more productive to direct that time and energy toward building a positive, trusting relationship with students; helping students understand the benefits of engaging in a particular activity or program; and using pedagogy that is active, engaging, and perceived by students as needs satisfying. If you focus on these three things, students will be intrinsically motivated, and you will eliminate the need for bribes and manipulation.

In summary, the following characteristics define an effective character or SEL program:

- *Professional development*: Teachers receive sufficient training to implement the program.
- *Sequencing*: A clearly identified step-by-step approach to knowledge and skills is being taught.
- *Explicitness*: Clearly communicated knowledge and skills are taught and assessed.

- *Direct instruction*: The program includes direct delivery of the curriculum.

- *Activeness*: Direct instruction is balanced by a multistrategy approach of engaging integration activities such as peer interaction, behavioral rehearsal, and role-play.

- *Curriculum integration*: The program is integrated into the academic curriculum.

- *Focus*: Sufficient time is devoted exclusively to social and emotional (character) skills.

- *Models and mentors*: The program provides opportunities for students to observe and work with positive role models and adult or peer mentors.

- *Parent and community involvement*: The initiative involves parents and community members and organizations in a coordinated approach to character development.

- *Intrinsic motivation*: The program appeals to students' intrinsic motivation to learn and grow, instead of relying on the traditional carrot-and-stick approach.

## This Book's Approach

### Relationships! Relationships! Relationships!

Everyone knows the first three rules of real estate: Location! Location! Location! Less well known, yet far more important, are the first three rules of education: Relationships! Relationships! Relationships! In my own experience, the most positive school experiences involved teachers I liked and respected and who I felt cared about me. Cohen (1999) agrees, stating, "Virtually all learning happens within the context of human relationships. . . . [T]he contacts we have with individual students affect how they feel about . . . what they are learning" (p. 17). As I tell teachers in my professional development workshops, if students like and respect you, and feel cared about and respected, they will learn anything you have to teach. And unless they are absolutely inspired by the content alone, if students don't feel liked or respected and don't like and respect you, they will not learn from you.

Ryan and Deci's (2002) research supports this view: "children who [feel] securely connected to, and cared for by . . . teachers [are] the ones who more fully internalize . . . positive school-related behaviors" (p. 19). Most important, often simply having a good relationship with a teacher or other adult at school can have a profound positive impact on students' social, emotional, and even physical well-being. "A . . . groundbreaking study (Klein, 1997) of over 12,000 adolescents found that parent-family connectedness *and connectedness to school* were protective factors against emotional distress; suicidal thoughts and behavior; violence; use of cigarettes, alcohol, and marijuana; and early sexual experimentation" (Cohen, 1999, p. 18).

Therefore, this book's approach is based on a foundation of positive, trusting student-teacher relationships. And because power in the classroom resides primarily with the teacher, it is his or her responsibility to initiate relationship building. Taking the time to get to know students at the beginning of the year and helping them get to know you are essential to teaching in general, but particularly to teaching social-emotional content. This approach is well worth the time and effort it requires: slowing down and building trust speeds up and deepens the learning in the long run.

Just how do you build these kinds of relationships with students? As Glasser (1998) says, "It takes a lot of effort to get along well with each other . . . [but] the best way to begin to do so is to have some fun . . . together. Laughter [and fun] are the foundation of all successful long-term relationships" (p. 41). After establishing some clear basic classroom expectations regarding rules, procedures, and so forth, explain the importance of developing trust in the classroom. You might tell your students that all new learning involves taking risks, and without trust, risk taking is not going to happen. Then play some team-building games and hold class discussions on topics that interest students. Tell them about yourself: your family, your interests, places you've visited, jobs you've held. Have students complete an interest inventory. Try to find a connection with each student. Greet them at the door each morning, attend their extracurricular activities, or sit with them at lunch. Hundreds of ways of showing students that you like them and care about them are possible.

One of the benefits of the interactive strategies in this book is that most of them serve double duty, developing social-emotional knowledge and skills and simultaneously building and deepening relationships. If, however, you find that students balk at participating in the activities, evaluate the relationship you have with them. As you know, some students, whether due to attachment issues in general, past experiences with teachers, or just their individual personalities, are more resistant to relationship building than others. Be patient, keep trying, and never give up on a student. He or she may be just testing you to see if you are sincere.

## What's In It For Me? (WIIFM)

Besides relationship building, a second important aspect of this book's approach is the emphasis on appealing to intrinsic motivation. Whatever they are being asked to learn, students need to know "What's in it for me?" (or WIIFM). I'm not referring to stickers, candy, pizza parties, or other rewards. Students need to understand how engaging in SEL or character development is going to add quality to their lives, both long-term and short-term. Holding class meetings on the benefits of demonstrating positive character in general and then on specific SEL skills (e.g., impulse control, delaying gratification, cooperation, etc.) will help them recognize why they are being asked to engage in character development, even if it isn't "on the test." In addition, because most students live in the present, they need to experience SEL teaching strategies that are engaging or needs satisfying. So as a student, even if I don't see an immediate need in my life for, say, empathetic listening, if I learn the skill through an active, novel, and enjoyable learning strategy, that alone will most likely be enough to internalize my motivation to participate and learn.

While most of this book's chapters include some direct teaching, each minilecture is accompanied by student-centered activities—games, skill practice, role-plays, and the like—that appeal to a variety of learning styles and personality types. Also, every activity and strategy in this book is designed to appeal to students' intrinsic motivation by appealing to one or more of their five basic needs (explained in detail in Chapter 3). Also, because SEL is inherently about them, students tend to find it intrinsically engaging. If you experience resistance to SEL in general or to a specific activity, and you've already evaluated your relationship with the resistant students, you might need to examine (1) how well you explained (or involved the students in examining) what's in it for them in the long and short term or (2) how engaging your teaching strategies are.

## Internal Control Psychology

Finally, as noted in the introduction, internal control psychology, specifically Glasser's choice theory (CT) and how it relates to social-emotional knowledge and skills, makes up the core content of the book. Generally, each chapter is devoted to one component of CT, including information that can be directly taught followed by activities designed to help students integrate and internalize the learning. The knowledge and skills build from one chapter to the next, incorporating and expanding on those previously learned. While CT is the principal theory investigated, I don't believe any one theory or model has all the answers, so throughout the book, I have included (and cited) ideas and strategies from a variety of other sources that expand and support choice theory. Through the information and skills presented in these chapters, students will gain the following benefits:

- An understanding of their locus of control
- An understanding of themselves and others' motivation
- An appreciation for their common humanity as well as for individual differences
- An understanding of how their perceptions form, and an appreciation for the role of perceptions in their lives
- An ability to recognize and identify their own and others' emotions
- An ability to regulate their emotions
- An ability to control impulses and delay gratification
- An ability to create a personal vision, set goals, and plan effectively
- Strategies to reduce stress and anger
- An ability to self-evaluate their behavior
- The ability to take others' perspectives
- The ability to experience empathy
- Social skills for a variety of social contexts
- Skills for building and maintaining relationships

Mastery, or at least competence, in these social-emotional skills is necessary for character development. Learning and applying these skills encourage and enable, among other important character traits, personal and social responsibility, respect, perseverance, self-control, compassion, and a strong work ethic.

## This Book's Approach Versus the Criteria for Effective Character or SEL Programs

Although *Inspiring the Best in Students* is not, in and of itself, a complete program, it does include many of the characteristics of effective character and SEL programs. It is *sequenced*, intended to be taught in a step-by step, chapter-by-chapter order; it is *explicit*, listing the specific knowledge and skills being taught in each chapter; it involves *direct teaching* (i.e., lecture) and *active* learning, using multiple engaging student-centered activities throughout; it encourages *curriculum integration*, explaining specific "curriculum connections" in each chapter; and it emphasizes *intrinsic motivation*, avoiding the traditional reward-and-punishment approach to motivation.

The final chapter suggests ways that schools might address the rest of the criteria for effective programs—namely, professional development, focus, modeling and mentoring, and parent and community involvement.

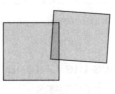

# 2 | A WORLD OF CHOICeS

An important prerequisite to bringing out the best in students is their understanding of some fundamental truths. One important truth is that *every human being experiences multiple influences*: our genes, our physical being, the culture(s) to which we belong, our friends and family, the media. First, our genetic makeup influences or predisposes us to a variety of things, including personality traits, such as being shy or extroverted; personal strengths and talents, such as athleticism or musical ability; and our mental and physical health (e.g., clinical depression and diabetes show strong evidence of a genetic link). Then there are physical influences. One's body type, height and weight, overall health, and physical appearance significantly influence one's choices and behavior. Third, we tend to assimilate the attitudes, behaviors, and values of the various cultures to which we belong, which include not only our national and regional cultures, but also our ancestral culture, our religious culture, and subcultures such as our work culture or that of our family and friends. We all know that as children approach adolescence, their peer culture strongly influences almost all aspects of their lives, while adults' influence tends to wane. Finally, the media, particularly television and the Internet, bombard us with more information and more attempts at persuasion than we've ever experienced before, profoundly influencing the way we think, communicate, and experience our world.

The second important truth is that *all human beings experience adversity*. Some individuals face more difficult obstacles than others, but no one is exempt from the multitude of challenges that life offers. Some of the toughest include chronic illness, extreme poverty, natural disasters, famine, political oppression, and war. Then, of course, there are physical, mental, and emotional disabilities and disorders; the loss of loved ones; divorce; economic recession; job loss; moving; relationship issues; and raising children. Finally, we all deal with day-to-day struggles, too: fatigue, family squabbles, traffic tie-ups, bills, car repairs, and more. The list could go on and on. I'm not trying to bring my readers down, but I believe it is important that students understand that no matter what they struggle with in life, they are not alone. We all face barriers.

The third truth is that no matter what influences we experience or what obstacles are in our path, *human beings ultimately have free will*. We may not be able to choose our parents, genetic composition, nationality, body, or many of the other influences we experience. Nor are we able to avoid adversity or even choose the kinds of obstacles we run up against. A choice we always have, however, is how we behave in response to the influences or adversity we experience.

We can choose to allow our influences or obstacles to control us, holding us back from achieving our goals, or we can do whatever is in our control to knock them down, scale them, or rise above them. Or if they truly are insurmountable, we can choose how we want to be and what we become within the parameters of our limitations. As author William A. Ward states, "Adversity causes some . . . to break, others to break records."

An extremely common response is that of the victim—to blame the influence or the obstacle in an attempt to excuse or justify her behavior or her life situation. After all, who wants to admit responsibility for doing something careless, irresponsible, or destructive, for failing to achieve a certain degree of happiness, for falling short of potential? There are lots of scapegoats. First and foremost, we blame other people:

- "Josh *made* me mad! I just *had* to punch him!"
- "That class knows just how to push my buttons! That's why I lost it and went ballistic in front of my ninth period class."
- "Everyone else smokes weed (copies homework, drinks at the after-prom party, cheats on taxes, etc.)."
- "My mom was always really critical of me. I guess that's why I can't be successful at anything I try. I just don't believe in myself."

In addition to other people, we often focus blame on inanimate objects, including various forms of technology:

- "It's not my fault I dropped the crystal bowl! That stupid chair was right in the way."
- "That six-pack was just sitting there in the refrigerator, begging me to drink it, Dad."
- "I'm sorry my paper is late; my computer crashed last night."
- "I couldn't text you that I wasn't going to be home on time. I must have been in a dead zone."

It is true that sometimes we have to maneuver around chairs, that leaving beer in the refrigerator when a teenager is home alone may not be a great idea, and that technology is sometimes unreliable. Therefore, in some cases, objects may well be the reasons for our behavior. In other cases, they may simply be convenient excuses. Nonetheless, these are not necessarily the *causes* of the behaviors. They may have been factors, but instead the underlying causes may well have been a tendency to hurry, in the case of the broken bowl; the teenager's lack of impulse control, in the beer drinking incident; a propensity to procrastinate, in the computer scenario; and irresponsibility, in the cell phone situation. It's much easier to blame something outside our control than something within ourselves.

Two other targets of blame are learning disabilities and psychological disorders. As with other factors that affect us, we can choose to allow these diagnoses and the labels that accompany them to control and limit us, or we can focus on what we can control and try to overcome them. It is not easy to overcome learning disabilities, emotional challenges, or mental disorders. But it is not hopeless. There are hundreds of examples of historical figures and contemporary celebrities who have done so and who can inspire others to follow their lead. For example, Albert Einstein, Thomas Edison, General George Patton, Walt Disney, Steve McQueen, Tom Cruise, and Henry Winkler are among the many famous people who overcame learning disabilities (www.learningrx.com); Vincent Van Gogh, Abraham Lincoln, Napoleon Bonaparte, Charles Darwin, Winston Churchill, Red Sox great Jimmy Piersall, singer-songwriter James Taylor, actress Carrie Fisher, and director Tim Burton have overcome depression or bipolar disorder (www.realmentalhealth.com). And obsessive-compulsive disorder (OCD) is said to have afflicted Michelangelo and continues to plague contemporary celebrities such as David Beckham, Donald Trump, Leonardo DiCaprio, and Howie Mandel (www.disabled-world.com). Despite the difficult, sometimes heartbreaking challenges these people face or faced, they have been able to make significant contributions to the world. They provide proof and inspiration that learning disabilities, mental disorders, and labels may challenge us, but they do not control our destiny—we do.

Along with other people, inanimate objects, technology, disorders, and disabilities, we have found other excuses for our behavior. Among the most popular are the following:

- Temporary physical or mood states ("When I'm tired and hungry, I just snap at people.")
- Birth order ("I have to be the center of attention; I'm the baby!")
- Heredity ("I'm not good with names. I'm just like my mom.")
- Ethnic stereotypes ("I hate to part with a dollar. I'm Scottish.")
- Learning styles ("I'm a kinesthetic learner. I just can't learn from Ms. Jones; she lectures all the time.")
- Parents ("I learned to be critical from my dad.")
- Physical attributes ("I'm just a dumb blonde.")
- Astrology ("Of course I have a bad temper. I'm a fire sign.")

Do things like birth order, heredity, and rearing influence our behavior? Of course. Furthermore, if we *believe* in stereotypes or that physical attributes or celestial bodies affect us, then they, too, become an influence. But despite these variables, we always have choices, even in the most difficult circumstances. Victor Frankl (1984), a survivor of Nazi concentration camps, writes, "In the concentration camps . . . we watched and witnessed some of our comrades behave like swine while others behaved like saints. Man has both potentialities within himself: which one is actualized depends on decisions but not on conditions" (p. 135). With an understanding of the learning objectives addressed in this chapter, students can take the first steps toward transcending life's challenges and learn to control their behavior even in the most difficult circumstances, thus taking personal responsibility for their own destiny.

## Teaching Students the Foundational Principles

CHARACTER OBJECTIVES: Students will gain information that will help develop personal responsibility, respect, compassion, optimism, and perseverance.

SEL OBJECTIVES: Students will gain information that will help develop self-awareness, awareness of others, and empathy.

PERFORMANCE OBJECTIVES: Students will demonstrate verbally or in writing an understanding that

- Every human being experiences multiple influences.
- Every human being experiences adversity.
- Human beings have free will—we have an *internal locus of control*, and we have the ability to choose our behavior despite our circumstantial influences and challenges.
- Every choice has a consequence: positive, negative, or neutral.

### Teaching Strategies

The following activities and discussions are designed to be followed in the sequence they are presented. The first two, Inside-Outside Circle and the class meeting, can be used for a variety of purposes and are referred to in subsequent chapters to meet other objectives. Therefore, before explaining the specific ways they can be used to meet this chapter's goals, I describe how to set them up and how they might be used generally. In addition to teaching students SEL, both of these strategies are excellent community-building activities.

### Inside-Outside Circle

This is an extremely flexible cooperative learning structure that can be used in a variety of ways in almost any classroom. The only requirement is enough space. The steps of Inside-Outside Circle (Kagan, 1994) are as follows:

1. Have students count off by twos.
2. Direct the 1s to stand in a circle.
3. Once they have arranged themselves in a circle, ask them to turn around so that they are facing out.

4. Now direct the 2s to face the 1s so that they create an outer circle.

5. Give the students a direction such as "Shake hands with the person you are facing and say 'Good morning!'"

6. Next, give the students a question or problem to discuss and a time parameter. For example, "For the next 2 minutes, discuss everything you know about the Civil War."

7. After 2 minutes is up, direct them to shake hands again and say, "Nice talking to you."

8. Direct one of the circles to move to the right or left a certain number of people. For example: "Outer circle, move three people to your right. Please say 'Hi' to the people you walk past."

9. Either give them the same question, or ask them to discuss something different.

10. Repeat steps 5–10 as needed.

You can use Inside-Outside Circle

- As an ice breaker or team builder. You might ask your students questions about topics like these:
  - Their favorite kind of music
  - Something they do for fun
  - A favorite food or dessert
  - Someone they respect or admire
  - A favorite movie, television show, or book
  - Something they wish people knew about them
  - A favorite song, musical group, rapper, or singer
  - Something they are proud of
  - Someone from history they would like to meet
  - A gift they would like to give the world
  - Something they are grateful for
  - Other topics of high interest to students

- As a way to help students discover prior knowledge about a particular topic before holding a large-group discussion.

- As a drill-and-practice activity. For example, give each student an index card with a different term or vocabulary word and its definition. During Inside-Outside Circle, have students check the understanding of the person opposite them and then rotate one of the circles. You might even have students switch cards with the person opposite them after each rotation.

- As a review. Each prompt could be to ask the students to review what they remember about a specific aspect of a lesson or unit they are about to be assessed on.

- As a listening exercise. Have the inner circle speak first for a minute or two about a particular topic. The outer circle can't say anything. Then have the members of the outer circle summarize what they heard their partner say. Then have the inner circle give the outer circle feedback on how accurate and complete their summary was. Then have the 1s and 2s switch roles.

The Inside-Outside Circle activity allows students a chance to consider and begin to articulate their own thoughts and to hear others' thoughts about questions they will be asked in the class meeting. Preparing students in this way leads to an engaging and meaningful whole-class discussion.

Before asking students to get into position for the Inside-Outside Circle, you might need to define the word *influence*. Tell the class that something that influences you is something or someone that has an effect on your thoughts, feelings, or actions. You might give a personal example, such as "Being tired or hungry has an influence on me: I tend to be less patient." Or, "My older sister influenced my taste in music. Because of her, I really like some of the old-school R&B artists like James Brown and Aretha Franklin."

Once you have succeeded in getting the students into the concentric circles, complete the following steps:

1. Have students greet their partners in some appropriate way.

2. Say, "We all experience influences that affect our behavior. Who are some of the people who have influenced you in some way, either

positively or negatively? For the next minute or two, talk to the person you are facing about them."

3. When the talk begins to die down, stop them, and invite them to shake hands and say something like, "It was good talking to you."

4. Direct the students in the outer circle to move two or three people to their right and greet their new partner.

5. Have them share their answers to the same question with their new partner. (You might repeat this process one more time or move on to the next question.)

6. Have the inside circle move two or three people to their right.

7. Say to them, "Not only people influence our behavior; sometimes things influence us, too. (Give them an example of something that influences you.) What are some things that affect your thoughts, feelings, or actions?"

8. Repeat this same question two or three times, making sure you have them greet each new partner, alternate the movement of the inside and outside circles, and say something appropriate to end each discussion.

After this discussion, students are ready to take part in the class meeting activity.

### The Class Meeting

This strategy has three major purposes: to create and maintain a sense of community in the classroom; to solve class problems; and to teach, integrate, and assess course content. Whatever the purpose, the structure and format are the same. Start out by having students sit in a circle (desks and chairs are optional) with no furniture in the way. This structure creates the sense that the class is a community of equals, with no one in a more powerful position than anyone else. It also allows for all students to make eye contact with the speaker without having to turn around in their seats. Some teachers use a specific part of the room for class meetings, possibly on a rug. Another possibility is to use a ball, talking stick, or other object that is safely and easily passed from student to student to designate the speaker. Once the students are seated in a circle, have students review the ground rules:

- The person with the ball (or other item) is the speaker.
- Listening to the speaker is the only acceptable behavior; no side conversation or interruptions are allowed.
- When the speaker is finished, he or she will pass the ball to someone whose hand is raised.
- No put-downs (verbal or nonverbal) are allowed.
- Anyone who wants to may participate.

The class meetings use a Socratic approach. The teacher's role is to formulate and ask thoughtful and engaging questions. One way to do so is by following the "define, personalize, and challenge" format. *Defining* questions simply clarify the term, concept, or problem that you are discussing. *Personalizing* questions ask students to relate the concept, term, or problem to their own life experience, helping them connect to their schemata or background knowledge. Finally, *challenging* questions ask students to use higher-level thinking skills through the use of application, analysis, synthesis, or evaluation questions.

For example, if the topic were a literary concept such as *conflict,* you might ask the following questions:

*Defining Questions*

- What, in your own words, does *conflict* mean?
- Is a conflict the same as a fight? How is it the same? How is it different?
- What are some different kinds of conflict that a person might experience?
- Can a person be in conflict with him- or herself? Explain.

*Personalizing Questions*

- What conflicts have you experienced personally?
- How does it feel to be involved in a conflict?
- Have you ever witnessed conflicts that others have experienced?
- How do people attempt to resolve their conflicts?
- What are some of the consequences or results of conflicts?

*Challenging Questions*

- Can conflicts be avoided? How?
- Should conflicts always be avoided? Why or why not?
- What are the best ways to resolve conflicts? The worst?

At first, it is a good idea to plan your questions, writing them down in your lesson plans or on a note card. As you become more comfortable with the class meeting format, you'll find it easier to develop questions as the discussion evolves.

Following are examples of specific uses of the class meeting to meet the objectives for this chapter.

## CLASS MEETING 1: INFLUENCES

*Defining Questions*

- Let's review. What, in your own words, is the definition of an influence?
- In general, what kinds of influences are there? (You might want to record a list of the kinds of influences students generate.) Answers might include people (family, friends, teachers, coaches, peer pressure, etc.), legal and illegal drugs, alcohol, genes, the media, technology, advertising, positive influences, and negative influences.

*Personalizing Questions*

- Who have been some influential people in your lives? How do you feel about their influence on you?
- Have you ever influenced anyone else? Do you think you had a positive or negative influence? How does it feel to have influence with others?
- Besides other people, what kinds of influences have you experienced?

*Challenging Question*

- Based on what you've heard in our class meeting, what generalizations or conclusions can we make regarding influences? (Hopefully, what will come out, among other things, is that we all experience influences from a variety of sources.)

(Note: If students go in a different direction than you'd hoped, you can redirect them using more closed-ended questions such as "Who experiences influences?" or "How many influences might a person experience in his or her life?")

### CLASS MEETING 2: ADVERSITY

(Note: You might substitute the word *adversity* with *challenges* or *difficulties* for younger students.)

*Defining Questions*

- What, in your own words, is adversity?
- What different kinds of adversity do people experience in life?

*Personalizing Questions*

- Do you know anyone who has experienced adversity? It could be someone you know personally or someone you know about, such as a historical figure or a celebrity.
- Have you ever experienced adversity?
- What kinds of adversity might you experience in your life?

*Challenging Questions*

- Should you expect to experience adversity? Why or why not? (This is where the learning objective that no one can escape adversity should come out.)
- What can you do, if anything, to prepare for adversity?

Because this meeting was not preceded by an opportunity for students to prepare their thoughts and comments (as in the Inside-Outside Circle preceding Class Meeting 1), you might have students turn to a partner and address each question each time before opening up the general discussion.

### The Fist

The Fist activity (Gossen, 1992) helps students understand the concept of the internal locus of control. Begin by explaining to students that they are going to participate in an activity that makes some important points about behavior. Next, pair students up. It's best if they are working with someone who is not a close buddy. After they have a partner, tell them they have 5 seconds to decide who is Partner A and who is Partner B. When time is up, have the As raise their hands, then the Bs, just to make sure they did as they were asked. Next, explain that you are going to give them all a job and that it is important that they all do their best at accomplishing the job. You might mention that the job doesn't require a great deal of effort or skill, doesn't hurt, and lasts only a minute. Then ask for a commitment that they will do the best they can to accomplish their task. Next, explain the tasks as follows:

> Partner A: Your job when I say "Go!" is to make a fist and keep it closed for one minute, no matter what. Don't use it on anyone. Just keep it closed. Any questions? Partner B: Your job when I say "Go!" is to persuade your partner to open his or her fist, using any means at your disposal, except you can't touch your partner, either with your own body or with another object. (That second part is for the young loophole finders: "I didn't touch my partner—the point of my pencil did.") Use your creative persuasive abilities. Think about what you do to get your parents or your brothers and sisters to do what you want. Any questions?

After you say, "Go," you might want to move around the class, monitoring behavior and listening for the kinds of strategies the students employ. After 1 minute, say, "Stop." Next, ask how many Partner Bs were successful in getting their partner to open his or her hand. A few hands might go up. Bring to their attention the low number of hands raised. Ask what strategies worked, and start recording a list. After you record the list of the successful strategies, ask the students to tell you the strategies that they tried. You will see many of the following persuasive strategies or attempts to influence:

| | |
|---|---|
| Asking | Nagging |
| Reasoning | Yelling |
| Telling | Threatening |
| Rewarding (bribing) | Lying |
| Appealing to the relationship | Verbally attacking |
| Negotiating | Punishing |
| Tricking | Humiliating |
| Reverse psychology | Physical intimidation |
| Guilting (shaming) | Physical force |

If you don't get as complete a list as you'd like, asking, "What else do people do to persuade or influence other people to do what they want?" will generate more external control strategies. After developing the list, ask the students, "What can we say about people and behavior based on this activity?" If this question is too open-ended, you might follow it up by asking, "Can your partner *make* you open your fist?" or "Whose behavior can you control?" or "What connections can you make between your partner's attempts to influence you and the other influences (and adversity) we experience in life?" With some discussion, you should be able to get consensus around the following two points: (1) People and other influences do not *make* us behave. If individual students opened their fist, it is only because they chose to open it; even if someone physically overpowers us, their influence is only temporary. (2) Therefore, we *choose* our behavior, even in the face of strong influences or adversity.

This activity will take students a long way toward understanding that they are in control of their behavior and that they are responsible for their choices. I recommend you follow the Fist activity with Class Meeting 3.

### Class Meeting 3: Freedom of Choice

I have learned that even the Fist activity does not convince all students that they choose their behaviors, for two main reasons. First, many students believe that they are constantly being told what to do and what not to do at school and at home. Second, if we have something or someone to blame for our choices, we are free from taking responsibility for our behavior. I have used this particular class meeting many times to help students understand that all behaviors are chosen and that all behaviors have consequences, whether positive, negative, or just neutral.

Ask students to turn to a neighbor and discuss all the things during a typical week that they *have* to do, both at school and at home. After a few minutes, pass the ball or other item around the circle and ask each student to share one thing that they discussed with their partner, while you list the things they mention on the board, the overhead, or on a flip chart. The list will include tasks like these:

| | |
|---|---|
| Taking a shower | Feeding the dog |
| Sleeping | Eating |
| Taking out the garbage | Mowing the lawn |

Watching little sister

Going to the bathroom

Going to softball practice

Breathing

Playing video games

Doing homework

Next, tell them that you are going to challenge their list. You might go right down the list and ask, for example, "Do you really *have* to take a shower?" The students will respond with a loud, choral "Yes!" and some giggles, but there are usually a couple students who will say no. "Isn't that interesting," you might say. "If we really *have* to take a shower, then everyone would have said yes. Is it possible to go a week and *not* take a shower? Do you think anyone has ever done that?" Some students will see the point and agree. If not, you might explain that in medieval Europe it was considered unhealthy to bathe too frequently. Bathing as infrequently (by modern standards) as once a week was considered far too often. You'll get some "Yucks" and some "Ewwwws" but persevere!

Ask, "Why do we feel like we *have* to shower every day?" Students will say something like, "If you don't, you'll smell bad!" "Right! There is a *consequence* that we want to avoid, but we don't *have* to shower, right?" Most will concur. Cross "Take a shower" off the list and move on.

You will meet less and less resistance as you go through the list. For each item, ask, "Is it possible for a person *not* to do it? Has anyone ever *not* done it?" If even one person has ever chosen not to do it, then it is a choice, not a compulsory behavior. Make sure you discuss the consequences of both doing and not doing the activities listed. A few items will survive your inquiry and remain on the list, involuntary physical responses like breathing ("If you hold your breath long enough, you pass out and naturally begin breathing"), sleeping ("Even with all the caffeine you can consume, your body will eventually take over"), and eliminating ("*Not* going to the bathroom—that's a choice"). Even eating is a choice. The consequences of not eating are dire, but doing so is still a choice some make (fasting, hunger strikes, dieting, etc.).

You may be treading on dangerous ground when you discuss that following rules, doing household chores, and doing homework are choices. You don't want to encourage students to make irresponsible choices, nor do you want angry phone calls from home the day after the class meeting. It is important to address the question "So why does it seem like we *have* to listen to our parents, follow rules, do homework, and so forth?" One reason, of course, is that doing these things is better than the negative consequences associated with not doing them. A question I've learned to ask is "So, if all of our behavior is a choice, why do we choose to listen to our parents, teachers, and coaches?" Many reasons will come out, but one that I try to emphasize is that we trust them and know that they have our best interests in mind.

I also like to extend the class meeting by asking, "Which feels better, to think 'I *have* to do something' or 'I *choose* to do something'?" Almost unanimously, students will tell you that it feels better to know that they are in control and not being controlled. I say "almost unanimously" because some students, no matter how many activities you do or class meetings you have, will choose not to accept the belief that they choose all of their behavior. They would prefer to think that they are controlled. That way, they don't have to take the logical next step: realizing that they are responsible for their behavior. You might use their resistance to bring home your point: "See, if I could make Jonathan behave the way I wanted, he would agree." Don't be discouraged if you don't get 100 percent buy-in. We all learn at different rates, and this is a difficult lesson for many, especially those who are accustomed to a highly structured, controlling environment. After this meeting, you might want to post the two main points of the discussion in the classroom: (1) All behavior is chosen. That is, we have free will and an internal locus of control. (2) Despite the influences and adversity we experience, we are responsible for our choices.

### Direct Instruction

After the discussions and activities above, a minilecture based on Figure 2.1 will help students synthesize what they have learned so far. This visual represents a human being. The size of the outside circle represents his or her personal growth, the degree to which someone is able to achieve his or her potential. The center of the circle, labeled the internal locus of control, represents that which a person can directly control—his or her attitudes, thoughts, and actions. Outside that circle are all the influences we experience in life. The perimeter of that circle, illustrated by the dark outer barrier, represents the adversity we encounter. On the one hand, if we focus our awareness and energy on the influences or adversity in our lives, our internal locus of control shrinks, as does our ability to achieve our potential, making the outside circle smaller and the outside barrier thicker. On the other hand, if we focus on what we can control—our attitudes, thoughts, and actions—our inner circle grows, external influences are diminished, the barrier representing adversity weakens, and our circle expands as we get closer to reaching our full potential, even in the face of adversity.

Students will need specific examples of individuals who have overcome adversity. You might use someone like Stevie Wonder as an example. He might have allowed poverty, racial discrimination, and blindness to limit his potential, but instead he focused on developing his musical ability, which not only helped him live a productive, happier life, but also gave the world the gift of his music.

## Curriculum Connections

The concepts of influence, adversity, and freedom of choice can easily be integrated into many content areas. Although these topics are most easily woven into English or language arts and social studies, they also can easily connect to health, family and consumer science, the arts, technology, and even math and science. Many scientists and mathematicians have influenced each other over the years, they influence us today, and many have overcome adversity to help us understand our world a little better. Furthermore, this material provides students with topics for writing, researching, reporting, integrating technology, and practicing higher-level thinking skills. You might consider designing the

**2.1   Locus of Control**

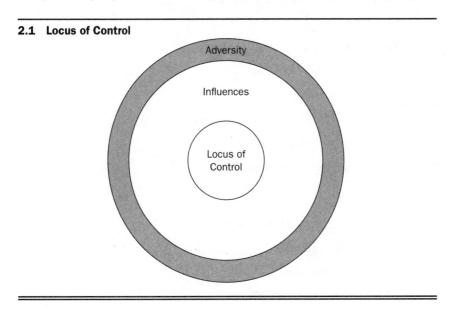

performance tasks described next to assess your students' understanding of the objectives of this chapter.

### Learning Journal Entries

A simple way of tying the SEL in this chapter with curriculum is to give students journal prompts throughout the unit. One way to do this is to have students answer the class meeting or Inside-Outside Circle questions in their journals before the discussions. Or you might ask students to simply write about what they learned during each class meeting, activity, or minilecture. Some of the journal entries might be developed into a final draft paragraph or essay—for example, their answer to the prompts regarding influential people, people they know who have overcome adversity, or adversity that they have experienced.

### Research Topics

You might ask students to research famous people who have overcome difficult obstacles. Some suggestions:

*Overcoming Physical Challenges*

- Itzhak Perlman—classical musician
- Michael J. Fox—actor
- Rick Allen—musician
- Lance Armstrong—bicyclist
- Ray Charles—musician
- Franklin Delano Roosevelt—U.S. president
- Helen Keller—author, speaker
- Ludwig van Beethoven—composer

*Overcoming Poverty*

- Frank McCourt—author
- Tina Turner—musician
- Bill Cosby—comedian
- Johnny Cash—musician

- Ringo Starr—musician
- George Foreman—boxer, entrepreneur

*Overcoming Learning Disabilities*

- Walt Disney—cartoonist
- Albert Einstein—scientist
- Alexander Graham Bell—inventor
- Tom Cruise—actor
- George Patton—U.S. Army general

*Overcoming Mental Disorders*

- John Forbes Nash Jr.—mathematician (as depicted in the movie *A Beautiful Mind*)
- Virginia Woolf—author
- Jimmy Piersall—baseball player
- Patty Duke—actress
- Isaac Newton—scientist
- Abraham Lincoln—U.S. president
- Howie Mandel—comedian
- Winston Churchill—British prime minister

*Overcoming Racial Discrimination*

- Barack Obama—U.S. president
- Sonia Sotomayor—U.S. Supreme Court justice
- Martin Luther King Jr.—civil rights leader
- Jackie Robinson—baseball player
- Rosa Parks—civil rights leader
- Frederick Douglass—author, statesman, abolitionist

*Overcoming Shyness*

- Lucille Ball—actress
- Tom Hanks—actor

- Mia Hamm—soccer player
- Bob Dylan—musician
- Orville Wright—inventor
- Theodore Roosevelt—U.S. president
- Eleanor Roosevelt—U.S. first lady

This list could go on and on. For other examples, see the following Web sites: www.learningrx.com/famous-people-with-learning-disabilities.htm www.darynkagan.com/overcoming/index.html www.realmentalhealth.com

A book students also might refer to is *Beating the Odds: A Teen Guide to 75 Superstars Who Overcame Adversity* (Snodgrass, 2008).

For content area teachers, you might have your students focus on famous people within your subject area (authors, scientists, artists, historical figures, athletes, mathematicians, Spanish speakers, etc.). Students might write a report about their chosen person, make an oral presentation to the class, or develop a DVD that documents how famous people have overcome difficult obstacles. Students might even be given an opportunity to create a class blog, beginning an online forum for celebrating human resilience.

### Inspirational Quotations

Assign students to research and write a written response to quotations about overcoming adversity. Or ask them to find a quotation that has special meaning to them and make a brief oral presentation about it. You might create an Inspirational Wall in your school or classroom with these quotes listed, called something like "Inspiration Station" or "The Wall of Scaling Walls." If your school has morning announcements or a regular television show, students might present an inspirational quote of the day or week.

An online search using "overcoming adversity" as the keywords results in several Web sites dedicated to inspirational quotations. For example, at the Web site http://quotations.about.com/cs/inspirationalquotes/a/overcomingad11.htm, students will find dozens of quotations, including the following:

- "Never, never, never, never give up."—Winston Churchill
- "Obstacles cannot crush me. Every obstacle yields to stern resolve. He who is fixed to a star does not change his mind."—Leonardo da Vinci
- "Obstacles don't have to stop you. If you run into a wall, don't turn around and give up. Figure out how to climb it, go through it, or work around it."—Michael Jordan
- "Others can stop you temporarily—you are the only one who can do it permanently."—Zig Ziglar
- "All the world is full of suffering. It is also full of overcoming."—Helen Keller
- "A certain amount of opposition is of great help to a man. Kites rise against, not with, the wind."—John Neal
- "Adversity brings knowledge, and knowledge wisdom."—Welsh proverb
- "A smooth sea never made a skilled mariner."—English proverb
- "A great pleasure in life is doing what people say you cannot do."—Unknown author
- "A dose of adversity is often as needful as a dose of medicine."—U.S. proverb

Students also might be assigned to combine this activity with their research topic, choosing a quotation, reporting about the person who said or wrote it, and describing what experience or event inspired his or her words.

## Discussing Benefits

This chapter has addressed foundational principles that are essential for students to understand before moving into more specific SEL. Before going on, it is important to establish with the students the benefits of SEL and character development. Students, like everyone, need to know why they are being asked to learn or do something. If students understand WIIFM and the teaching strategies are engaging, you will find that they will enthusiastically participate in SEL. If students are not buying in, it is likely that (1) there is a relationship or trust issue, (2) they don't see the value in what they are being asked to learn, and/or (3) the pedagogy is not engaging. An excellent way to help students see the value and benefits of SEL is through a class meeting. Here are some questions you might include in a class meeting to help students understand how SEL will add quality to their lives:

*Defining Questions*

- What does the word *success* mean?
- Are there different kinds of success?
- What do you think are the characteristics of a successful life?

*Personalizing Questions*

- What are some of the successes that you have experienced so far in your life?
- How does if feel when you are successful?
- Would you like to get that feeling more often?
- What success would you like to experience this week? This year?
- What kinds of success would you like to have in life?
- Do you know someone whom you consider successful?

*Challenging Questions*

- What did it take for you to achieve the success that you have?
- What do you think it took _____ to be successful?
- Do you think you'd experience more success if you were more _____ ? (Fill in with attitudes and character traits that students mention.)
- What kinds of things do we do in school that help you be successful?
- If I told you I wanted to teach you some information and skills in class that would help you have more success in your future, would you be interested in learning it?

## Conclusion

This chapter is primarily about creating awareness in students of fundamental principles before attempting to teach them more sophisticated social and emotional skills. In a society that sometimes seems to encourage blaming our choices and problems on everything from other people to the position of the stars, it is important that they accept the message that despite the various influences and adversity we all encounter, they always have choices: "You can steer yourself in any direction you choose." Their locus of control is within them, and every choice they make will have a consequence. And the sum of their choices is their destiny.

Through these understandings, students begin to take responsibility for their own behavior and gain empathy for other human beings, who, like them, struggle with difficulties and obstacles in life. Through learning about famous people who have overcome adversity, students appreciate the importance of putting their energies into their locus of control instead of allowing their situation or other obstacles to limit them. They also learn the importance and power of optimism and perseverance.

## Reality Check

Students' understanding of the ideas in this chapter (or the book in general) doesn't mean that they will suddenly all take personal responsibility for their actions. Lickona and Davidson (2005) refer to the Head, the Heart, and the Hand of character development. Almost all students seem to readily learn and understand (the Head) the knowledge and skills involved in character education or SEL. Many sincerely express the desire (the Heart) to demonstrate responsibility, respect, compassion, fairness, honesty—to do the right thing—but probably just as many, when faced with an ethical decision, will make the more self-serving choice. The Heart and the Hand, which represent consistently behaving in ways that demonstrate ethical principles, present more difficult challenges. I often hear parents and teachers say, "He knows better! Why doesn't he behave better?" Or "She knows the difference between right and wrong. Why does she make so many wrong choices?" There are a couple of reasons. First, like any new learning, SEL takes modeling and guided practice to the point of automaticity. A class meeting on the *internal locus of control* will not transform all students. At first, they need to hear, see, and talk about the internal locus of control regularly and frequently. Individual conversations with students can relate to the ideas through the language the teacher uses. Asking questions like "Is this something within your control?" "What choices do you have?" or "What do you think the consequences might be if you make that choice?" help keep the ideas alive in students' minds.

Another reason that it is difficult for many students to make the transition from just Head and Heart to Head, Heart, and Hands is that they have had many years of other, possibly less effective patterns of thinking and behaving, which have become like well-lubricated neural superhighways in their brains. These well-established habits don't disappear overnight. However, with ongoing support and encouragement from trusted adults, they can continuously improve, sometimes in small increments, but sometimes in leaps and bounds. Over the years, I've known many teachers say things like "He's like a different kid from 2 years ago when he was in 3rd grade" or "She has come a long way since September." With patience, intentionality, persistence, and an eye constantly on the quality of your relationship with them, you can help add the Heart and the Hand to the Head and, in so doing, positively influence even the most resistant and challenging students.

With these foundational principles in place, we can begin to gain a greater understanding of what within us is driving our behavior. In the next chapter, we will examine the five components of intrinsic motivation that drive all of our choices.

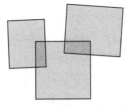

# 3 | INTRINSIC MOTIVATION AND THe FIVe BASIC HUMAN NeeDS

Much of the 20th century was dominated by behaviorism. In the behaviorist school of thought, a person's locus of control is in the environment, external reinforcement being the main influence on human learning and behavior. Another name for this kind of thinking is *external control psychology*. Although it still enjoys quite a bit of popular acceptance, external control psychology has largely been reconsidered and replaced in the academic and scientific community by internal control psychology, the psychology of the 21st century.

The development of internal control psychology, the belief system based on the assumption that all behavior is aimed at satisfying internal needs, began in the second half of the 20th century. In the 1950s, Harry Harlow's well-known experiments with baby Rhesus monkeys demonstrated the intrinsic need for physical affection and the direct relationship between the satisfaction of that need and the monkeys' physical health (Blum, 2002). Since Harlow, other theorists have focused on the components of intrinsic motivation, or basic human needs. Some of the best-known internal control theorists include James (1892/1962), Alderfer (1972), and Maslow (1943), best known for his hierarchy of needs. More recently, researchers Ryan and Deci (2002) and Thompson, Grace, and Cohen (2001) have contributed significantly to the field of internal control psychology.

Whereas Harlow focused on the importance of love and affection as a basic need, these other researchers and theorists have posited a variety of basic needs. There seems to be general concurrence on three basic needs sets: the *physiological needs* for food, water, warmth, and safety; *relatedness needs*, the needs for positive, trusting human relationships; and *power needs*, which include the needs for competence, achievement, personal growth, and recognition.

## Choice Theory

Choice theory (Glasser, 1998) is the internal psychological model that provides the foundation for this book. I selected choice theory over any other version of internal control psychology for three reasons. First, Glasser's five basic human needs include the three basic needs sets mentioned earlier and two others that seem particularly important to students: freedom and fun (explained in detail later). Second, choice theory offers a clear, comprehensive explanation of human behavior, which is valuable to educators in helping students develop emotionally, socially, and academically. Finally, I have personally taught choice theory and related concepts to thousands of educators and students around the world, and I find that people easily grasp the concepts and related skills and can immediately put them to use in their classrooms, schools, and personal lives.

This chapter focuses on the five basic human needs that are the root cause of all human motivation. An understanding of the needs helps students

- Gain a greater understanding of themselves through an understanding of the underlying source of their behavior, their happiness, and their frustrations;
- Learn to assess their behavior in terms of its effectiveness, in both the short term and long term;
- Self-evaluate their behavior in terms of its alignment with principles such as responsibility, self-control, kindness, and honesty;
- Choose new, more effective, more responsible behaviors based on their self-evaluation;
- Better understand others' behavior, gaining greater tolerance, acceptance, and empathy.

In addition to these benefits, understanding the basic needs also gives students tools that enable them to analyze and understand characters in literature and history, thus connecting to the core academic curriculum as well.

## Glasser's Five Basic Human Needs

One of the main tenets of choice theory is that *all behavior is purposeful*. When I first heard those words during a school district conference day, I had to stifle a chuckle. I'd been supervising the cafeteria during lunch for a number of years, and "purposeful" was not the word I would have used to describe much of the 7th and 8th graders' behavior. Later on, I learned that when Glasser says "purposeful," he doesn't mean productive or consciously goal oriented; he simply means that there is an underlying purpose for all behavior. That is, we are doing the best we can to meet our basic human needs given the knowledge, skills, and resources in our repertoire of behaviors. If we could think of a better way of achieving this purpose at any given time, we would choose it.

After I understood this basic premise, I gained insight into the source of my students' behavior—the five intrinsic needs:

1. To feel physically good and emotionally safe,
2. To have friends and feel accepted,
3. To feel a sense of competence and importance,
4. To experience independence, and
5. To laugh and play.

Glasser labels these needs, respectively, *survival, love and belonging, power, freedom*, and *fun*. As you read about each of these needs, think about its significance not only to your students but also to your own life.

### The Physical Need: Survival

Physical needs are often the first thing to come to mind when considering basic needs. However, because human beings have the ability to imagine the future, we also think about our future security and wellness. So the need to survive, while primarily physical, has a psychological component: our need for a sense of order and security, now and in the future.

Students' survival need, like that of adults, is concerned with physical drives like food, shelter, and rest; but whereas adults' security is often focused on financial stability, students are much more concerned with physical and emotional safety in the present, both at home and at school: in the hallways and the cafeteria, on the bus and the playing fields. We will discuss the implications of this need and the four psychological needs regarding students' behavior later on in this chapter.

## The Four Psychological Needs

Human beings require more than just physical well-being in order to lead happy, fulfilling lives. We have psychological needs as well. As you read about each of the following, I invite you to think of the people, activities, things, and places in your life that help you satisfy each of your psychological needs.

### Love and Belonging

Humans, like many other species, are social creatures. We live in family units, work on teams, form social and civic organizations, attend social gatherings, and engage in hundreds of other behaviors that require cooperation. Almost all human endeavors have some social dimension to them. Having a strong need for love and belonging is one of the reasons the human species has been so successful. In our primitive past, humans' urge to belong to a group manifested itself in cooperative hunting, gathering, child care, and defense of the group, behaviors that were essential to the other need we just discussed, survival.

It is well-known that newborns require a certain amount of physical affection in order to thrive. In his 1999 book *Love and Survival,* cardiologist Dean Ornish concludes that there is a lifelong connection between the quality of our relationships and our physical and mental well-being. Citing hundreds of studies, Ornish says about the power of love and belonging, "I am not aware of any other factor in medicine—not diet, not smoking, not exercise, not stress, not genetics, not drugs, not surgery—that has a greater impact on [our] quality of life" (pp. 2–3). Studies such as those cited by Ornish support the choice theory principle that the deep-seated urge to love and belong—to connect with others, to cooperate, and to give and receive affection—is truly a basic need with a profound influence on our overall physical and mental wellness.

### Power

Power is the most frequently misunderstood need. For many people, the word *power* is synonymous with dominance, authority, or control. Because people don't like to think of themselves as being domineering or overly controlling, many do not like to admit they have an intrinsic need for power. When understood in choice theory terms, however, the concept of power takes on a much broader, more positive meaning. In general, power involves competence, personal growth, knowledge, skills, achievement, having a voice, making an impact, and gaining recognition. The drive to gain power ultimately manifests itself in what Maslow refers to as *self-actualization*.

There are three general ways people behave as they attempt to meet their need for power:

- *Power over.* Closest to the common perception of the word *power*, this is exercising one's influence over something or someone. A sculptor exercises *power over* her medium. The guitarist demonstrates *power over* his instrument. A mechanic exhibits *power over* an engine. It is when people use (or abuse) power over other people irresponsibly that we see power in a negative light. Fortunately, many have used their influence with people for the greater good: Gandhi, Martin Luther King Jr., Mother Teresa, and scores of everyday heroes who use what power they have to help others. Many educators are in their ranks.

- *Power within.* Gaining *power within* refers to personal growth—developing the knowledge and skills that increase the quality of our lives. Gaining power includes learning, achieving success, and enjoying the feeling of self-worth that accompanies personal growth. Without the need for the *power within*, human beings never would have developed the culturally and technologically sophisticated world we live in today.

- *Power with.* Power with refers to the power achieved when working cooperatively with others. It is the place where the need for power and the need for love and belonging intersect. If you think of the great achievements of the human race, they all resulted from humans working together or building on the achievements of others before them.

Students' need for power manifests itself in many ways, such as achieving academically, excelling in sports, participating in the arts, and holding positions in student council. As we will discuss later in the chapter, the need for power often shows itself in less responsible, sometimes destructive ways. Helping students understand their need for power and how they can direct it in positive ways has important implications regarding the kind of people they become.

### Freedom

Glasser includes a need for freedom, which finds support in the research of Ryan and Deci, who refer to a need for autonomy. Although few theorists refer to a basic need for freedom or autonomy, it is hard to imagine freedom not being an innate human need. Consider the number of individuals throughout history who have suffered or died in a struggle to achieve independence and self-determination.

The need for freedom can be divided into two major types:

- *Freedom to.* This involves having choices: freedom to go where you want, say what you want, associate with whom you want, pursue an interest or a career, and so on. We are most aware of the need for freedom when we perceive it as being threatened. Think of a time when you were pressured into doing something or going somewhere you didn't particularly want to. A good deal of the frustration you feel in that kind of situation is your *freedom to* need tugging at you.

- *Freedom from.* This aspect of the freedom need refers to freedom from things that cause us physical or emotional discomfort, such as fear, stress, disrespect, or monotony. In classrooms, much of the *freedom from* need is provided for if there is a safe, structured, stimulating learning environment developed through the teacher's use of effective instructional and management strategies.

### Fun

Glasser proposes a fifth need that is particularly important to children and therefore to education: the need for fun. A seemingly simple concept, fun is difficult to define. What is considered fun for one person (solving a crossword puzzle with pencil and paper) might significantly differ from what is fun for another (playing videogames on a Wii). Fun seems to be most obviously manifested through various forms of play and through laughter and humor. Although fun may at first seem trivial in comparison to other needs, research from zoology and medicine suggests that play and humor are as necessary to human development and wellness as love and belonging, power, and freedom.

Most scientists agree that play has two main functions: (1) "rehearsing and honing of behavior important to adults" (Hawes, 1996, p. 2) and (2) "strengthen[ing] bonds between group members" (p. 3).

Children's play may well serve the same important functions. Glasser relates fun to learning: "Fun is the genetic reward for learning. We are descended from people who learned more or better than others. The learning gave these people a survival advantage, and the need for fun became built into our genes" (1998, p. 41). Although the need for fun seems to be most important in childhood, people need to play all their lives. The purposes of play in adults are more likely to be for social bonding, reducing stress, and remaining physically and emotionally healthy (Hawes, 1996). Play is essential for learning and adds to our physical and emotional well-being, but it also is a wonderful tool for building relationships.

## Important Characteristics of the Five Basic Human Needs

Although it is important for students simply to understand what needs are driving them, a thorough understanding of the characteristics of these driving internal motivators can potentially enable students to successfully develop (or transform) themselves and the important relationships in their lives.

First, the needs are *innate*. Another term for *basic human needs* would be *genetic instructions*. Just as other species have behavioral instructions as part of their genetic makeup, so do humans. Because of our well-developed cerebral cortex, humans' genes are not shouting instructions like "Fly south!" or "Go to sleep!" or "Swim!" Our genes are whispering things like "Be physically comfortable and safe," "Connect with others," "Gain personal power," "Be free," and "Have fun!" We have free will in how we choose to behave (or not behave) in following these genetic instructions. It is not a choice, however, for human beings to feel the urge to survive, love and belong, gain power, be free, or have fun. These needs are in our genes.

Although needs are *universal*, people have them in *varying degrees*. In other words, all human beings have all five needs, but each of us does not experience the same amount of drive for each need. For example, a person with a high need for love and belonging might spend a great deal of time and energy on relationships, both in his personal life and at work. He—let's call him Dan—might attend social events, join clubs and civic associations, enjoy close relationships with friends and family, and enjoy his favorite activities most often in the company of others. A person with higher power and freedom needs—call her Sheryl—might spend more time alone, working on projects, reading, attending courses, competing in athletics, constantly learning and achieving. Sheryl may have a few close friends, but she may not spend as much time with them as Dan spends with his.

In choice theory terms, Dan and Sheryl have different *needs profiles*. A person's needs profile, the relative quantities of the five basic needs by which an individual is genetically motivated, does not dictate a person's behavior, but it is a powerful influence. The examples with Dan and Sheryl are not necessarily the way individuals with high love and belonging or power needs behave. They are simply ways these two individuals might manifest their particular needs profiles. The concept of the needs profile is so important that the next chapter is devoted entirely to it, exploring how it can affect students' personalities, behavior, and interpersonal relationships.

Another important characteristic of the needs is that they often *conflict* with other people's needs. If, for example, a store manager has a high need for power and meets that need through frequently exerting what authority he has, he might easily come into conflict with an employee with a high freedom need. A classroom of students with a high need for fun and freedom might end up "in trouble" with a teacher who has a high survival need (order and security). I'd like to stress that in each of these cases, the individuals involved *might* come into conflict. It is not inevitable. People attempting to meet their different needs (or even the same need) in the same environment don't necessarily end up at odds. One of the purposes of this book is to discuss how to teach students ways they can meet their needs effectively without coming into conflict.

## Responsible and Effective Behavior

Although all behavior has a purpose, to meet one or more of our basic human needs, all behavior is not necessarily effective or responsible. The term *effective behavior* refers to a behavior that works for us; it satisfies our need(s). The term *responsible behavior* refers to behavior that satisfies our need(s) without depriving others of meeting theirs. Unfortunately, not everyone chooses effective and responsible behaviors all the time. As every teacher knows, students find thousands of ways of behaving irresponsibly. This book is dedicated to helping students turn those behaviors around. First, let's look at how each need can drive irresponsible behavior.

### Survival

When the survival need is at risk, the brain shifts into the *fight-or-flight response*. In schools, the kinds of "flight" behaviors students choose are wearing coats and pulling hoods up to hide their faces, physically isolating themselves in the very back of the room, skipping classes, or skipping school altogether. Others have developed coping skills and defenses that may put others at risk. This is the "fight" response. These students may disrupt class, showing how tough and cool they are; they may engage in verbal or physical bullying or encourage others to do so; and some join gangs.

### Love and Belonging

In school, the necessity of a structured classroom environment, the demands of the curriculum, the constant movement from class to class, and the vast populations of many schools make it difficult for students to have opportunities to form relationships, to socialize, and to feel part of a group. This sense of isolation leads some students to engage in relatively benign, though still irritating, behavior like chatting during class, sneaking text messages, or secretly calling each other on cell phones. Some students still engage in that old standby, writing notes to each other. If this sense of isolation extends beyond students' school day, more serious, sometimes dangerous behaviors might emerge, such as irresponsible sexual behavior or gang membership—and none of us can forget the tragedy caused by those isolated students who took refuge in the "trench coat Mafia" at Columbine High School.

### Power

The primary purpose of education is to meet the need for power. Ironically, while students find it fairly easy to meet their power needs in extracurricular activities (e.g., sports, music, drama, art, etc.), many find their need for power highly frustrated in the academic domain. These are students who don't achieve the degree of success many of their classmates do. Some have been labeled as failures, underachievers, or at risk. Indeed, many are at risk. Because these students find it difficult to satisfy their need for power by achieving *As* and *Bs* in their classes, they figure out other ways of being successful and making an impact on the world: finding success at "being bad," by disrupting their classes, upsetting their teachers or classmates, bullying weaker students, smoking, vandalizing the school, gaining a reputation for being a big partier or for being sexually experienced, or by joining a gang.

### Freedom

Students need to make choices and to experience novelty. When asked where they feel free in school, many will respond, "Nowhere!" or "At lunch." When students are frustrated in meeting their freedom need, some of the irresponsible behaviors they use in an attempt to achieve freedom include clowning around, disrupting class, and daydreaming. Extremely frustrated students may resort to shutting down and sleeping through classes, skipping classes, using illegal drugs, or dropping out.

### Fun

The need for laughter, enjoyment, and pleasure is rarely, if ever, met all by itself; it is usually met in combination with another need or needs. It's fun to be with people you like (love and belonging), to do things you do well (power), and to do what you choose (freedom). You might even say the need for fun is met to some extent any time you effectively meet another need. Therefore, if students are not able to play and experience fun in school in responsible ways, they will use many of the irresponsible behaviors already discussed: from passing notes, clowning around, and disrupting class to skipping school, bullying, and using drugs.

## Encouraging Effective, Responsible Behavior

Students have figured out innumerable ways of meeting their needs irresponsibly in school. These behaviors are not going to go away overnight. That's the bad news. The good news is that we can dramatically reduce irresponsible behavior in school in two ways. First, we can deliberately create a needs-satisfying classroom and school environment. We can be more intentional about our teaching strategies, considering questions such as these:

- How can I create a place of safety, order, and physical comfort?
- How can I develop positive, trusting relationships in my classroom and school?
- What can I do to help my students be successful, gain recognition, and feel like their voices are heard in my classroom?
- How can I provide students with choices and novelty on a regular basis?
- How can I bring play, laughter, and fun into the classroom?

My book *The Classroom of Choice: Giving Students What They Need and Getting What You Want* (Erwin, 2004) explains almost 200 management and instructional strategies for achieving a needs-satisfying environment.

Second, we can teach students information and skills that will help them choose more effective, more responsible behaviors. People can (and most are more than willing to) choose new responsible behaviors if they are at least as needs satisfying as their former irresponsible behaviors. One story immediately comes to mind. When I was a staff development specialist, I organized a group of students called the Choice Players. I trained them in choice theory, and then they made presentations at workshops and conferences about the importance of developing positive teacher-student relationships and creating a needs-satisfying classroom environment.

At one of our conferences, the 1999 Quality School Consortium conference in Boston, Dr. Glasser was the keynote speaker. Hearing that a group of students was in the audience, he invited them up on stage in front of about 500 educators. He asked the students, "Why should kids learn about internal control psychology and the five basic needs?" Several of the students gave testimonials about how learning choice theory had helped them have better relationships, make more responsible choices, and stay out of trouble in school. But I'll never forget one student, a high school senior named Juan Pablo. He told about his gang membership and how he didn't know it at the time, but the gang met all of his basic needs. (I had no idea he was a gang member when he first joined the Choice Players.) He said during the training he went through that he did a lot of thinking and figured that in the long term, gang membership was going to lead to jail or an early death, as it had for so many of his friends and extended family. He gradually decreased his involvement with his gang and got back into modern dance, something he'd practiced and loved for years before his gang affiliation. His ending remark, "I figured dancing could meet all of my needs for love and belonging, power, freedom, and fun and isn't going to get me killed or incarcerated," was met with a standing ovation. I stood in the back of the auditorium with tears in my eyes. The last I heard about Juan Pablo was that he'd gone to a state university and majored in dance.

Not every student's story is as dramatic as Juan Pablo's, but an understanding of internal control psychology can help young people understand the source of their behavior and can help them learn to take more effective control over their lives. The best place to start this process is to teach students about their five basic needs.

## Teaching Students the Five Basic Human Needs

CHARACTER OBJECTIVES: Students will gain information that will help develop responsibility, respect, tolerance, acceptance, and compassion.

SEL OBJECTIVES: Students will gain self-awareness, awareness of others' motivation, empathy, self-evaluation skills, and the ability to self-motivate.

PERFORMANCE OBJECTIVES: Students will demonstrate verbally or in writing their understanding that

- All behavior is motivated from within by one or more of the five basic human needs.
- The five basic needs are the need for survival, love and belonging, power, freedom, and fun.
- We meet our needs in two general ways: responsibly and irresponsibly.

## Teaching Strategies

I have used all of the following strategies to teach students about their five basic human needs. Students generally grasp the ideas easily and immediately make connections to their own lives. You probably won't use all of these strategies with your students. I'd encourage you to choose, modify, or add to these teaching approaches based on what you know about your students, their personalities, and learning styles.

### Journal Entry/Class Discussion

A good way to lead into a lesson on basic needs is to ask students to individually reflect on what they think they need (as opposed to want) in order to be physically and emotionally satisfied or happy. You might ask them to write their ideas in a learning journal and then have a large-group discussion.

During the class discussion, you could record all their ideas. Later on, after you have given the minilecture on the five basic human needs, you might engage the class in categorizing the things they listed under the five basic needs. Students may find that one item might be perceived to meet different needs for different people. For one student, listening to an iPod is simply a recreational escape (freedom and fun); for another student, who is an aspiring guitar player, it is an essential tool for learning new songs (power).

### Minilecture

Once your students have experienced the Fist and class meeting activities described in Chapter 2 and understand that no one can make them behave, that all behavior is chosen, the next step is to explain to them that *all behavior is purposeful*. The purpose of all behavior is to meet one or more of five basic human needs that everyone is born with. Explain each of the needs, using the following definitions and synonyms:

- *Survival*: the physical need to eat, drink, seek shelter and physical comfort, and be safe
- *Love and belonging*: the need to form and experience positive relationships at home and at school, to be accepted, to be part of a group
- *Power*: the need to achieve, to experience success, to learn, to receive recognition, to be good at something, or to be listened to (*Note*: Emphasize

the difference between this definition of power and the one they may have previously known.)

- *Freedom*: the need to experience independence, to make choices, and to seek novelty
- *Fun*: the need to play, to laugh, and to experience pleasure

Although this book is aimed for teachers of grade 3 and higher, many teachers of younger children have also taught the five basic needs to their students, using symbols to help their nonreaders and early readers understand the concepts. They might use an apple or some other food item to represent survival, a heart to represent love and belonging, a star for power, a bird or butterfly for freedom, and a smiley face or rainbow for fun. Symbols also work well with English language learners.

Once students have gained a basic understanding of the definitions of the basic human needs, it is time to help them to make personal connections.

### The Needs Circle

This activity is a great way of helping students personalize and integrate their knowledge of the five basic human needs. First, referring to Figure 3.1, ask

**3.1  The Needs Circle**

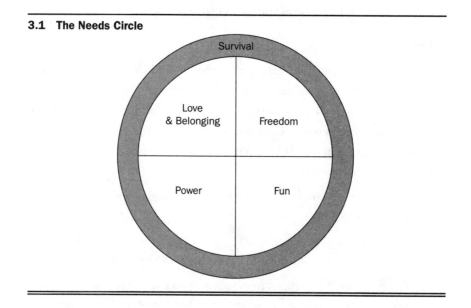

them to list in the outer Survival circle the names of people who provide them with some of the physical essentials: food, clothing, safety, and security. Then ask them to list the places or things that help them survive and be physically healthy. You might give them some examples: a winter coat, a house, running sneakers, the YMCA. Finally, have them list some activities that they engage in that help them take care of themselves physically. Again, give them some examples (e.g., eating healthy snacks, exercising, sleeping eight hours a night, etc.). Explain, too, that the same people, places, things, or activities will probably go in more than one part of the Needs Circle.

Next, ask students to list the following in the four quadrants of the inner circle:

LOVE AND BELONGING

- People whom they feel connected to (names of family, friends, etc.)
- Things and places that help them feel connected (school, church, Instant Messenger, cell phone, etc.)
- Activities that create a sense of belonging (playing team sports, playing in a band, hanging out with friends, etc.)

POWER

- People who teach them important skills, listen to them, help them learn, or give them recognition (parents, teachers, coaches, friends)
- Things or places that help them improve their knowledge or skills (playing fields, books, musical instrument, soccer ball, computer)
- Activities that they want to learn or be skilled in (music, drawing, sports, etc.)

FREEDOM

- The people around whom they can really be themselves
- Places and things that help them feel free (vacation spots, their bedrooms, the Internet, favorite comfortable clothes)
- Activities that create a sense of freedom (listening to music on headphones, taking walks, shopping, reading)

Fun

- People who make them laugh or are fun to be around
- Places and things that help them have fun (video games, the mall, the beach, books)
- Activities that are fun for them (playing games, going to a great pizza place, traveling, etc.)

A variation of this activity would be to use, instead of concentric circles, a graphic organizer made up of outlines of the five symbols used to describe the needs (e.g., apple, heart, star, etc.).

### Class Meeting on the Quality World

After the students have completed their Needs Circles, holding a class meeting is a good way to help them understand that while we all have the same basic human needs, there are significant differences in the ways we meet them. This awareness of the common humanity that underlies an amazing diversity opens the door to greater understanding of others, which in turn leads to tolerance, acceptance, compassion, and eventually appreciation.

Begin by structuring the class meeting and setting the ground rules as explained in Chapter 2. Next, before launching into the class meeting itself, explain that the people, places, things, and activities that students listed in their Needs Circles are part of what choice theory calls our *Quality World.* The Quality World, a "small, personal, internal world, which each person starts to create in his or her memory shortly after birth and continues to create and re-create throughout life, is made up of a . . . group of specific pictures that portray, more than anything else we know, the best ways to satisfy one or more of our basic needs" (Glasser, 1998, pp. 44–45). Explain that while our basic needs are the same, our Quality World pictures are different. Our Quality World is like a personal picture album in that whenever we find a new, highly needs-satisfying "picture," we add it to our album. The album changes as we change. Sometimes we take pictures out, and sometimes we replace one picture with another.

Next, explain that the first series of questions are to be answered in a WHIP (without hesitation immediate participation) format. You'll ask a question and hand the ball or other item to the student to your right or left. That student will answer the question with a word or short phrase and pass the ball to his or her neighbor. The ball and the discussion "whip" around the circle until the ball gets back to the teacher. After the first question, the teacher asks another, sending the ball in the opposite direction. For this part of the class meeting, ask questions like these:

- What is one person, place, thing, or activity you listed under Survival?
- What is something you listed in the Love and Belonging quadrant?
- What is one way you meet your need for power?
- How do you meet your need for freedom?
- What do you do for fun?

Next, explain that you'll be asking more open-ended questions—questions that require more thinking and longer responses. Explain that anyone who wants to answer may ask for the ball:

- What do we learn about the basic human needs and the Quality World from this discussion?
- How are we alike? How are we different?
- What would it be like if we all had the same Quality World pictures? Explain.
- How do people, places, things, and activities get into our Quality Worlds?
- Which is better, a small Quality World or a large one? Why?
- How do we create a bigger Quality World for ourselves?

Answers will differ, of course, and you may have other questions that will be generated from the class meeting, but from a well-directed discussion, students will gain a greater understanding of both the universality of the basic human needs and the diversity of our Quality World pictures. They will understand that an individual's Quality World pictures are a reflection of his or her gender, age, culture, and life experience. They will also gain an appreciation for the diversity of our Quality Worlds and will understand how and why to increase the number of pictures in their Quality Worlds.

### Quality World Collage

This activity is another way of helping students integrate the concept of the basic human needs by relating the needs to their own lives. It can also provide a medium for them to learn about, understand, and appreciate others' Quality Worlds.

A week or two before you begin this activity, start collecting magazines, lots of them. Ask the students to bring their old magazines in, ask faculty members to bring in theirs, and visit the school librarian to see if there are any old magazines he or she would be willing to donate. Music, sports, fashion, and youth-oriented magazines are best, but any will do.

Once you have a good supply of magazines and have taught your students about the basic human needs and the Quality World, explain that their assignment is to create a collage that represents some of the important people, things, places, and activities in their Quality Worlds. Provide each student with a sheet of poster board, scissors, and a glue stick, and tell them that their job is to choose pictures out of the magazines that represent ways that they meet each of their five basic needs. Also, explain that they will be presenting their Quality World collage to the class when they are finished.

Remember to discuss what kinds of pictures are appropriate for a school project. The rule of thumb might be any picture that they would not be embarrassed to show their mother, a member of the school board, or the school principal.

### More Class Meetings

While engaging in the activities described thus far increases students' self-awareness and understanding of others, it is important to hold class discussions, like the one following the Needs Circle, to expand the learning that can be derived from them. Here are some other topics related to the basic human needs:

- Discuss how students meet their needs now is different from when they were younger, and how their Quality World pictures will change as they become adults.

- Discuss responsible and irresponsible ways that they observe people attempting to meet each of the needs.

- Read a story or novel, and then discuss the needs that characters are attempting to meet throughout the narrative. Evaluate whether the behaviors the characters choose are effective and responsible.
- Similarly, bring in a newspaper or newsmagazine and discuss current events by looking at the needs that people are attempting to meet.
- Watch a film clip or TV show and discuss the needs portrayed.

### Classroom Needs Circle

This discussion not only helps students understand and apply the concept of the basic human needs to their lives, but also gives them an opportunity to have a say in the development of classroom rules. After a short review of the definitions of the needs and the difference between responsible and irresponsible behavior, pairs or small groups of students complete a T-chart for each basic human need (see one done for power in Figure 3.2). On one side, students list specific behaviors that would enable them to meet each of their psychological needs (love and belonging, power, freedom, and fun) in *responsible* ways in the classroom. On the other side, students list ways that they think students might attempt to meet their needs in *irresponsible* ways in a classroom setting.

**3.2   T-Chart for Power**

| Power | |
|:---:|:---:|
| Responsible | Not Responsible |
| | |

Next, lead a whole-class discussion, coming to consensus on a list of behaviors derived from those developed in the pairs or small groups. After consensus, write the responsible behaviors agreed on inside the appropriate quadrants of a circle like the one shown in Figure 3.3. Also write the irresponsible behaviors outside the circle.

Once the Classroom Needs Circle is completed to everyone's satisfaction, post it on the wall so that students can refer to it frequently and use it to help self-evaluate their behavior. The Classroom Needs Circle should be thought of as a living document, which can be amended at any time in an ongoing effort to attain a match between the teacher's and students' Quality World pictures of a classroom and reality.

## Curriculum Connections

The content of this chapter not only is useful to students emotionally and socially, but it also can provide a springboard for many language arts, social studies, and science lessons and performance assessments. I will attempt to address developmental considerations, but you are the expert on your students. Please consider how you might use or modify each of the following ideas to fit your class's developmental level and to align with the standards and assessments for which you and your students are responsible.

**3.3  The Classroom Needs Circle**

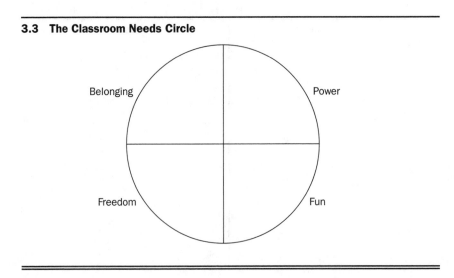

### English Language Arts

PARAGRAPH WRITING: Students might write a series of paragraphs on how they satisfy each of the five basic needs, referring to the Needs Circle graphic organizer for the people, places, things, and activities to include in the body of the paragraph.

ESSAY WRITING: Students could easily add an introductory paragraph, some transitions, and a concluding paragraph to develop the paragraphs from the preceding activity into a coherent report. They also could write an essay describing and explaining their Quality World collages, possibly focusing on themes that seem to emerge (sports, music, pets, technology, etc.).

ORAL REPORT/LISTENING PRACTICE: Students could present their essay or PowerPoint presentation while students, individually or in pairs, develop two or three "quiz questions" about the information presented to check their peers' listening-for-understanding skills afterward. This activity could easily be developed into a game, too, by assigning points for correct answers or for questions that stump the audience. This combination provides opportunities for the reporter to engage in public speaking, the class to practice listening and questioning skills, all to get to know their classmates better, and the class to have fun while learning useful skills.

LITERARY ANALYSIS: Students might analyze characters in a story, novel, or film through a choice theory lens. In cooperative groups of three or four, they might be assigned a character to track throughout the narrative, documenting that character's actions and thoughts. Then, they would discuss and hypothesize as a team the motivation behind the character's behavior in terms of the five basic needs. They might also evaluate the character's behavior in terms of responsibility (compassion, honesty, or other character traits that might be significant to the plot or theme). They could go on to identify the character's Quality World pictures (or ultimate goals). Often a protagonist in a longer work of fiction undergoes an important character change. This change is indicated by new behavior and sometimes different needs driving the behavior, represented by different Quality World pictures or goals. If the character is meant to be sympathetic or likable, as the protagonist almost always is, generally the behavior (after the change) and Quality World picture align with and illuminate the major themes. If the character is meant to be unlikable, the character's Quality World pictures generally contradict, and thus help illuminate, the theme.

A good elementary-level example is Disney's *The Lion King*. After his father is murdered by Scar, Simba runs away and lives with Timon the Meerkat and Pumbaa the Warthog. His behavior is driven by survival, freedom (from danger but also responsibility), and fun (a common phrase in the story is *hakuna matata*—"no worries"). After his character change brought on by reconnecting with his childhood best friend, Nala, Simba returns to his pride, which has suffered under the tyranny of Scar; avenges his father's murder; and takes his place as the rightful king. Here, the driving basic needs are freedom (this time freedom from fear), love and belonging, and power. Simba's Quality World pictures include loyalty, personal and social responsibility, love, and compassion, the main themes of the film. I've used a similar approach with middle school students in novels such as *Where the Red Fern Grows* and *The Outsiders* and at the high school level with *One Flew over the Cuckoo's Nest* and *King Lear*. In my experience, this approach will work with any good literature. The main developmental differences involve the reading level, which is addressed by choosing grade-appropriate reading material, and the amount of guided practice needed before letting the students work independently. Note that giving groups class time to analyze their characters allows you to provide needed support and differentiate instruction and helps prevent intergroup conflict.

### Social Studies

HISTORICAL ANALYSIS: Students can analyze events in history or current events through the lens of the five basic needs. Middle and high school students might be asked to write an analysis of the behavior of individuals or nations in terms of the primary needs their actions or words addressed. For example, during the American Revolution, the American patriots could be said to be focusing on their freedom and survival (economic) needs, while King George was driven by power (control) as well as survival (economic).

Younger students might choose a famous historical figure from the worlds of politics, religion, the arts, sciences, or another field; research what that person was famous for; and connect what he or she did to the five basic needs. For example, Martin Luther King Jr.'s civil rights struggle was about helping African

Americans gain freedom and power. Lyndon Johnson's Great Society program was aimed at helping raise people out of poverty (survival). P. T. Barnum and Charlie Chaplin both provided entertainment (fun) and made a fortune (survival and power) at it. Gandhi helped free India from British occupation (freedom, love and belonging). Other examples include Napoleon, power; Mother Teresa, love and belonging; Nelson Mandela, freedom and power; and Marie Curie, survival.

### Science

ANIMAL BEHAVIOR: Ask students to explore how animal species share one or more of humans' basic human needs. Or assign students to report on the specific genetic instructions certain species have.

### Technology

POWERPOINT PRESENTATION: Ask students to develop a PowerPoint presentation of the information in their Needs Circle or Quality World collage, possibly including video clips of their favorite movies or TV shows and audio clips of their favorite music.

BLOGGING: Students might create a weblog that encourages them to share the ways they meet their basic needs and invites students from other parts of the world to share the ways they satisfy their needs. Students would find commonalities with kids around the world, while simultaneously learning about other cultures. (This activity also gives you an opportunity to discuss and monitor safe and responsible blogging, making sure to advise students not to reveal personal information and to report anything that they feel uncomfortable with.)

### Visual and Performing Arts

MUSIC: Assign students, in small groups, to find music that represents the different needs and to make a class presentation. You might have each group find musical works that represent each need, or assign different groups one specific need and have them create a CD or playlist including works from different genres (classical, jazz, pop, country, etc.) that represent that need. They might develop a PowerPoint slide show to accompany their presentation.

DRAMA: Have students write and perform skits that express how the needs motivate our behavior. In small groups, students might be assigned one of the five basic needs on which to base a short play or skit. Or ask them to write an allegory in which the main characters represent each of the basic needs involved in some kind of conflict.

ART: Students might create a sculpture, drawing, painting, or other visual representation of the basic needs or the needs in conflict.

DANCE: Students could represent the needs, or conflict between the needs, through movement.

### Business

ADVERTISING: Invite students to analyze how TV, the Internet, or print advertisements try to appeal to the basic human needs. Then assign students a product to sell, asking them to create an advertisement that appeals to as many of the five basic needs as possible.

## Conclusion

Teaching students about the five basic human needs, the genetic instructions that drive all human behavior, can have a profound positive influence on students. First, knowing specifically what they need to feel happy, fulfilled, and in balance is the first step toward achieving those goals. Second, understanding that there are many ways of meeting their needs, some responsible and some irresponsible, helps students self-evaluate and make more intentional choices. Finally, realizing that all human beings have the same needs encourages a deeper understanding of others' behavior. This knowledge and understanding can help students self-evaluate, restrain impulsivity, behave more responsibly, and ultimately gain compassion. It also provides teachers and students with a common way of thinking and communicating, enhancing the whole school environment.

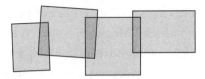

# 4 | THE INTERNAL PROFILE

In Chapter 3, we learned about the five basic human needs, or genetic instructions, that drive all human behavior. Although all human beings have all five needs, we do not seem to experience each need with the same intensity. Glasser (1998) states that what people call *personality* "is, in part, written into our genes. . . . What gives us our different personalities is that our five basic, or genetic, needs differ in strength" (p. 91). Glasser's term for this phenomenon is "genetic needs-strength profile" (p. 92). I prefer to refer to it more simply as our *internal profile*. Just as each human being has a unique physical or external profile, each of us has a unique internal profile, a slightly different combination of the relative strengths of the basic needs.

Similarly, just as our internal profile itself is unique, two individuals with similar internal profiles may demonstrate very different outward behavior as they attempt to satisfy their internal needs. For example, one person with a high need for power may tend to behave in a very controlling way, taking charge when she is in a group, being rather autocratic and demanding, and micromanaging the people around her. Another person with just as high a need for power may manifest that need by being achievement oriented, setting difficult goals for himself, holding himself to high standards, and working hard to achieve those goals and meet those standards. The needs, being such a general source of motivation, manifest themselves in a wide assortment of human behavior.

---

*Note:* The information and activities is this chapter are beyond the developmental ability of most 3rd graders. Reading this chapter offers benefits to you as an adult, but if you work with students younger than 4th graders, I wouldn't recommend attempting this mini-unit unless you modify it significantly.

An important consideration regarding the internal profile is that although we often focus on an individual's highest need, people experience the other four needs in their own personal hierarchy. Moreover, a person's least intense need may have as significant an impact on his behavior as his highest need. A person with a high freedom need whose lowest need is power will almost certainly behave differently from someone whose lowest need is survival. The first person may manifest his high freedom need in less challenging but safer ways than the latter: spending time alone surfing the Internet, collecting thousands of tunes for his MP3 player, gaining both *freedom from* and *freedom to*—freedom from mundane problems and freedom to listen to anything he chooses. The person with the low survival need may seek freedom in riskier ways, traveling alone to a new place, for example, or motorcycling or skydiving. Thus, two individuals with the same high need may behave very differently and may have significantly different personalities, due to the relative strength of other needs.

## The Internal Profile: So What?

The possible variations in the relative strengths of the five basic needs are seemingly endless. What does this have to do with education, particularly character education or SEL? A great deal. Students' understanding of their own internal profiles can help them develop important self-evaluation and self-regulation skills. Teaching that others have differing internal profiles is an excellent way to help students understand and celebrate human variation. Understanding leads to tolerance, then to acceptance, and ultimately to empathy and compassion.

## Teaching Students About the Internal Profile

CHARACTER OBJECTIVES: Students will gain information that will help develop respect, tolerance, and compassion.

SEL OBJECTIVES: Students will gain information that will help them develop self-awareness and awareness of others, an understanding of their own strengths and weaknesses, an ability to self-evaluate, an appreciation of diversity, empathy, and a basic social understanding that different people prefer different kinds of interaction.

PERFORMANCE OBJECTIVES: Students will demonstrate verbally or in writing

- An understanding of the definition of *internal profile.*
- An understanding of their own internal profile and its influence on their behavior.
- The strengths and challenges of their own internal profile.
- An awareness of others' internal profiles and ways they manifest themselves through behavior.
- An understanding that our internal profiles are not good or bad, just different.
- An understanding that, as we interact with others, knowing the concept of the internal profile can help us understand others' motivation for their behavior and choose more effective and productive ways of communicating with them.

## Teaching Strategies

In my experience leading hundreds of students through the following process, I find that students thoroughly enjoy learning about their own and others' internal profiles. Using the process and the sequence described in the following direct instruction unit, students will discover for themselves much of what I have explained thus far. This short unit begins with a minilecture and moves into active mode.

### Step 1: Define Internal Profile

First, explain the concept of the internal profile, saying something like this:

Remember when we learned that we all have five basic human needs? (Ask students to list them and write them on the board.) Having these five needs makes us similar. One of the things that make each of us unique is called our *internal profile.* We all have a unique external or outside profile. This is mine. (Turn sideways and show them yours. I like to stand right in front of my LCD projector and show my profile on the screen.) No one else's profile is exactly like yours or mine. Similarly, we all have a unique internal profile. A person's internal profile is the varying strength of each need that a person experiences. For example, Laverne may have a high need for love and belonging and a lower need for power. Ali may have a high need for power and a lower need for love and belonging. Can you see how Laverne's and Ali's internal profiles would influence their behavior? If they were on the same softball team, for example, Laverne might enjoy being a member of the team, the friendships, and so forth, as much as she enjoys winning games. Ali, on the other hand, might be playing more for the thrill of competition, working hard at improving his game, and enjoying the recognition that accompanies his success. How else might their behavior or their personalities be different? (Maybe write their responses on the board.)

Let's contrast another pair of differing internal profiles—maybe a brother and sister, for example. Sister Samantha has a high need for freedom and fun and a low need for power, while her brother Brandon has a high need for survival and a low need for fun. Their family is visiting Six Flags. How might their behavior be different? (Again, record this.)

This topic usually stirs students' interest, and they start guessing their own and their classmates' internal profiles. Tell them that they are going to engage in a process that will help them learn about their internal profiles and what that means to them individually, to the class, and to their relationships with friends, family, and others.

### Step 2: Descriptors Assessment

Provide each student with five index cards and ask them to write the five basic needs on the cards in large letters, one need per card: survival, love and belonging, power, freedom, and fun. Explain that you are going to read general descriptions of five internal profiles. Tell them that most likely none of the descriptions will fit them perfectly, but some of the descriptions will be more like them than others. Their task is to compare their personalities to the descriptions you will read. Remind them that they are looking for descriptions that match they way they *are*, not necessarily the way they would like to be. Next, read the following descriptions, projecting them simultaneously onto a screen as a visual aid, and ask the students to place their survival card on their desk and to hold the other cards in their hands. Also, explain that it is important that they listen actively.

### High Survival Profile

I like to feel safe and secure. I try to avoid taking big risks. I like order and organization, and I prefer my surroundings to be clean and neat. I enjoy knowing what is going to happen during my day. I get a little stressed if I don't. I also like to follow a fairly regular routine. I think about my physical health. I try to eat well and think it's important to take care of myself. People like that I am disciplined, well organized, and dependable.

Next, direct the students to listen to another description and to hold onto their cards until after you've read the entire description and given further directions.

### High Love and Belonging Profile

I am a people person. Relationships are my highest priority. I value personal warmth and close friendships. My thoughts are often about the well-being of my friends and family, and I like to spend lots of time with them. I enjoy social and family gatherings, and most of my favorite pastimes involve being with other people. I really don't like being alone. I try to reach out to others when they are sad, lonely, or just in need of a helping hand. People like the fact that I am a caring, friendly, and cooperative person.

After you've read this description, say, "If this description is more like you than the first, place your love and belonging card on top of your survival card. [You might need to demonstrate.] If it is less like you than the first, place your love and belonging card below the survival card. Remember, it doesn't have to fit you 100 percent. You should be looking for general similarities. Now, I'm going to read another description. Remember to wait until you've listened carefully to the whole description before you place your card."

### High Power Profile

I am a high achiever. I like to be good at things. In fact, often I like to be the best. I set goals, have high standards, and work hard to meet or exceed them. I believe people should do their best to reach their potential in life. I enjoy healthy competition, in school or at home. I am proud of my accomplishments and enjoy the recognition that they sometimes bring. I also enjoy being a leader. People respect me for my skills, accomplishments, and high standards.

After you have read this description, say to the students, "If this description is more like you than the others, place the power card above them. If it is less like you, put it below. If it is more like you than one but less than the other, place it between them. [You might need to demonstrate again.] If you think you have a tie, it's also OK to place two cards side by side. But first, do your best to order them most like you to least like you. OK, now I'm going to read a fourth description, so please listen carefully."

### High Freedom Profile

I love my independence. I like to have the freedom to make choices at home and at school. I really don't like it when people try to tell me what to do or control me. I enjoy trying new things and welcome change. I love traveling to new places and spending time outdoors. I value my solitude; some of my most treasured time is time spent doing something alone. I like the saying, "Think different." I consider myself to be quite creative. People like that I'm a unique individual and respect me for not being easily swayed by popular opinion or peer pressure.

As you did after reading the High Power Profile, direct the students to place their freedom card above, below, or between the survival, love and belonging, and power cards. Then say, "There is one more description. Please listen carefully."

### High Fun Profile

To me, life is all about laughter and fun. I try to bring a sense of playfulness to everything I do, and I try to liven up even the most boring tasks. I love doing things on the spur of the moment, and sometimes I'm a little disruptive at home or in school. I love games, celebrations, festivals, and parties. I have a great sense of humor and like to make others laugh. People like me because I'm energetic, funny, and just plain fun to be around.

After reading the last description, direct the students to put their fun card where it belongs in their arrangement. Next, have the students number their cards *in pencil*: 5 is the most like them; 4, next; then 3, 2, and 1, finally, as the least like them. Also, explain that there is another step to discovering their internal profile. It is called the Word Cluster Assessment. Tell them that it is a little more complicated, but it will help them get a more accurate picture of the strengths of their needs.

### Step 3: The Word Cluster Assessment

Some teachers think that the preceding activity, Steps 1–2, is enough to get the objectives of this chapter across to the students. I prefer to have more data on which to base the assessment and administer the Word Cluster Assessment. Make copies of (or re-create) the Word Cluster Assessment in the Appendix. Read the directions slowly to the students, checking for understanding as you go. I won't repeat them here, but you may need to clarify, for example, the difference between a row (horizontal clusters) and a column (vertical). Other tips before your students start their Word Cluster Assessment:

- Go through the vocabulary, checking for understanding.
- Remind your students that they must have a 5, 4, 3, 2, *and* 1 in each row.
- Also remind them that they are to assign a 5 to the word cluster that is *most* important to them. Tell them that if two of the three words in a word cluster are very important to them, but one is less important, they can ignore the one "off" word and go with the other two.
- Model the assessment by making a transparency and doing one row for the class. Remind them that this is an individual decision and not to let your choices influence theirs.

Now give them some time to work on the assessment as you circulate around the room.

### Step 4: Scoring the Word Cluster Assessment

There are a couple ways you can score the Word Cluster Assessment. The first way requires a color printer or copier. Using this approach, you would create a colored Word Cluster Assessment Scoring Key to give to your students.

For example, all the word clusters related to the love and belonging need might be red; to power, pink; to freedom, blue; to fun, green; and to survival, black. Explain to students that they are to add up the numbers that they have entered in the spaces before all the similar-colored word clusters. Once they have done the addition, they put their scores in the appropriate spaces on the sheet. Then they can list the needs in order at the bottom of the sheet from highest to lowest. (If they have a tie, put two needs on the same line.)

The second way to score the Word Cluster Assessment, which doesn't require a color printer, is to provide each student with a table like the one illustrated in Figure 4.1, directing the students to add the numbers they assigned to each word cluster designated in each box of the table. (*Note*: It might be easier for students to work in pairs: one student reading the row and column information while the other does the addition, then switching roles.) After performing the addition, students should follow the same process as explained for the other method, putting their scores in the appropriate spaces and listing their needs at the bottom.

If some students note a discrepancy between the results of the Word Cluster Assessment and the Descriptors Assessment from Step 2, allow them to choose which assessment they believe more accurately represents their personality.

### Step 5: Processing the Results—Homogeneous Groups

The next two steps are the most important parts of the internal profile process, where most of the learning and integration occurs. First, have students raise their hands according to which need turned out to have the highest score

**4.1 Black and White Scoring Key**

| Love & Belonging Word Clusters | Power Word Clusters | Freedom Word Clusters | Fun Word Clusters | Survival Word Clusters |
|---|---|---|---|---|
| Row 1: Col 1 | Row 1: Col 2 | Row 1: Col 3 | Row 1: Col 4 | Row 1: Col 5 |
| Row 2: Col 3 | Row 2: Col 5 | Row 2: Col 1 | Row 2: Col 4 | Row 2: Col 2 |
| Row 3: Col 4 | Row 3: Col 5 | Row 3: Col 3 | Row 3: Col 1 | Row 3: Col 2 |
| Row 4: Col 1 | Row 4: Col 4 | Row 4: Col 3 | Row 4: Col 2 | Row 4: Col 5 |
| Row 5: Col 2 | Row 5: Col 1 | Row 5: Col 3 | Row 5: Col 5 | Row 5: Col 4 |

for themselves: survival, love and belonging, power, freedom, or fun. Divide the groups up by highest need, sending them to different parts of the classroom.

If any one group is too large, see if there are any members of that group who had a tie for their highest need or a close second (within a few points on the Word Cluster Assessment), and ask them to work with students from that group. Quite often, the love and belonging group is by far the largest. With middle school students, it is often the fun group.

Next, designate (or have the group select) students to take on the following roles:

- *Facilitator*—keeps the group focused on the task.
- *Recorder*—writes the group's answers on chart paper.
- *Reporter*—reports the group's answers to the whole class.

Ask students to answer the following questions and to develop a poster that conveys their answers in any way they choose. Question 4 is where the students start to have some fun with the internal profile. I've listed quite a few items for them to relate to their highest need. For time's sake, you may want to limit the number, or you may want to come up with more. When coming up with answers, it's important that the students be able to explain why they chose the things they listed.

1. What are three strengths that people with your highest need demonstrate?
2. What are three challenges that people with your highest need demonstrate (or may be perceived by others)?
3. What is one strength people from the other high-needs groups demonstrate?
4. What song would best represent people with your highest need? (Singing this song is encouraged during the report out.)
5. What movie?
6. TV show?
7. Sport?
8. Vehicle?

9. Recreational activity?

10. Animal as a mascot?

11. Color?

12. Smell?

13. Footwear?

14. What is a slogan that would represent your group?

15. What group gesture would represent your strongest need? (Remind students this must be an appropriate gesture.)

16. What attitudes and behaviors do people with your highest need want from the people they live and work with? What do you *not* want?

After the groups have had time to answer the questions and create their posters, hang the posters on the wall and have the groups report out to the whole class, making sure to celebrate each group as it completes its presentation. During this portion of the processing, you might want to discuss avoiding "profile bashing," the tendency for one group to make disparaging remarks about another.

It is interesting to observe the various internal profiles working together, because the groups often manifest their highest need. For example, the love and belonging group will generally work well together; but if it is a large group, it may find it difficult to limit the answers to Questions 1 and 2 to only three, not wanting to leave anyone's ideas out. The survival group may be cautious, checking in with you to see if the answers are what you are looking for. The power group will have no doubt that the answers are correct, but the students may argue among themselves over which answers are the best. The freedom group may ignore some of your directions ("We decided not to list three strengths; we only wanted two."). The fun group may either go off task frequently or hurry through the assignment so the students can do something more fun.

Also, the posters the groups develop usually exhibit their characteristics. For example, the fun poster is quite often very colorful and humorous. Watch for these manifestations and point them out; they give credence to the whole concept of the needs profile.

### Step 6: Processing the Results—Mixed Groups

Next, develop groups of four to six students, making sure these groups have students from as many of the previous high-needs groups as possible. (Ideally, you would have groups of five, one student from each of the high-needs groups.) Again, assign the three roles: facilitator, recorder, and reporter. Then ask groups to come up with answers to the following questions, writing their responses on chart paper.

- What are the benefits of having people with a variety of internal profiles working together?
- What might be some of the challenges?
- How can we overcome the challenges?

Next, have the groups present their answers to the class. The answers will vary, but the students will make some important points. Regarding the benefits of a variety of internal profiles working together, students will often make statements like these:

- It's more interesting that way.
- Different points of view bring more ideas to the table.
- We're better able to play to our strengths.
- The group will be more balanced and more effective (love and belonging can balance freedom; fun can balance power, etc.).

Regarding the challenges, students will typically list responses like these:

- Sometimes it's hard to understand each other.
- We can become impatient or frustrated with each other.
- One particular high need that is difficult to get along with is _____.

Here are some students' ideas about ways to overcome challenges:

- Just being aware of different people's internal profiles
- Being open-minded
- Communicating their needs
- Being allowed to play to their strengths

### Step 7: Processing the Results in a Class Meeting

The last step to the internal profile process is to follow up the students' presentations with a class discussion of the implications of understanding the concept of the internal profile. You might ask the class the following questions:

*Defining Questions*

- What, in your own words, is a person's internal profile?
- How would you say a person's internal profile shows itself?
- Do you think a person's internal profile can change? Explain.
- Does a person's internal profile control that person or just act as an influence?

*Personalizing Questions*

- How might someone who observed you for a day determine your internal profile?
- What are the implications of your internal profile to you?
- Does your internal profile ever benefit you? Explain.
- Does it ever cause your problems? Explain.

*Challenging Questions*

- How can you use your awareness of your internal profile to make important choices in school, at home, and at graduation?
- How might you use your awareness of the internal profile in your relationships with others? (Discuss present as well as future relationships.)
- How can you use your knowledge of your internal profile to reach your professional or personal potential?

## Curriculum Connections

### English Language Arts

WRITING ASSIGNMENTS: Ask students to write an essay about their internal profile, using one of the following prompts:

- Describe your internal profile. How do your interests and behavior align with your internal profile?
- How is your internal profile like or different from the one of another member of your family? What are the implications of these similarities or differences?
- Compare and contrast your internal profile with that of one of your friends. What are the implications of these similarities or differences?
- What are the benefits and challenges that your internal profile presents to you in general?
- Write a poem that describes your internal profile.

LITERARY ANALYSIS: Ask students to analyze literary characters using the concept of the internal profile. Here are some possible directions:

- After having read a short story or significant portion of a novel or play, analyze a particular character's internal profile, supporting your conclusions with details from the text.
- Compare and contrast two major characters' internal profiles, using textual support for your major points.
- What character in the novel has an internal profile most like (or unlike) yours? Explain and support with details from the text.
- Describe a major character's internal profile. Explain what need or needs the character is attempting to meet through his or her behavior, and categorize the behavior as responsible or irresponsible.
- Read a poem and analyze the internal profile of the speaker or persona.

CREATIVE WRITING: Have students write an allegory using the basic needs as the names of the main characters.

### Social Studies

HISTORICAL ANALYSIS: Students can gain a clearer understanding of the motivation and personality of historical figures through analyzing their internal profiles. The following are some assignments you could give students:

- Assign individuals, pairs, or small groups of students to write or present an analysis of a historical figure's internal profile, supporting their analysis with facts (e.g., the historical figure's writings, quotations, actions, etc.).

- Ask students to write or make a presentation explaining how a historical figure's internal profile is like their own.

- Make the point that like individuals, nations can be seen to have internal profiles. Ask students to take two nations in conflict, and then compare and contrast the nations' internal profiles at that time, again using concrete support for their opinions. Examples: England and the American colonies during the American Revolution; Germany and the Soviet Union in World War II.

- Assign any of the above activities, but use current figures or events instead of historical ones.

### Mathematics

RELEVANT DATA: The data you gain from individuals or classes of students are relevant; they are about the students. And you can use the data gained from students completing the internal profile assessment in a variety of ways.

- Assign students to create different kinds of graphs that depict both their own individual needs profiles and the data compiled from a whole class of students regarding the highest or lowest needs.

- Assign students to find the percentage of students in the class whose highest need is fun (for example).

- Develop probability questions based on the internal profile statistics. For example, if a student from a particular class was randomly selected, based on the class data, what is the probability that that power is her highest need?

- Have students create a spreadsheet using the class data from the Word Cluster Assessment.

### Technology/Business

Have students create an advertisement recommending a person with their internal profiles to prospective employers (with disclaimers for some of the challenges of the internal profile). Alternatively, have students create an advertisement for someone with a different internal profile.

### Visual and Performing Arts

VISUAL ARTS: Have students create a work of art that demonstrates a particular internal profile or expresses the concept of the internal profile in some way.

DANCE: Ask students to perform an interpretive dance representing different needs in motion.

MUSIC: Ask students to

- Create a presentation of music that might appeal to different internal profiles.
- Write and perform a song or rap about their internal profiles or a piece of music that expresses one or more profile(s).

DRAMA: Have students create and perform a skit that demonstrates the concept of the internal profile.

### Technology

Have students

- Include their internal profile information on their MySpace or Facebook pages.
- Create a Web site that provides information on their internal profiles.
- Develop a blog devoted to their basic needs and internal profiles.
- Create a PowerPoint presentation on the concept of the internal profile.
- Create a CD mix or playlist of songs that represent their needs profiles.

## Conclusion

The concept of the internal profile is relevant to both students and teachers. From the small- and large-group discussions about the internal profile, you will find that students gain a deeper understanding of themselves and others. One of my 8th grade students, Rehema, a very popular girl, told me that she had been "freaking out" because she hated going to all the parties that she and her fraternal twin sister Kalekwa were invited to. She thought there was something wrong with her because Kalekwa just loved going to parties, dancing, flirting with boys, and staying up late. After Rehema learned about her internal profile, she was relieved. "I have a high need for survival and power," she said. "Kay is all freedom and fun. That explains why she loves parties, and I think they're so boring! I just didn't understand why I didn't have any fun. Now I can just let it go and do what I really like, which is to stay home and read."

An appreciation of the internal profile not only helps students understand who they are but also can have an impact on their future choices. A former English student, Tamiko, was a senior who had been planning to attend a two-year college and major in computer programming, which was really more her parents' goal than her own. Tamiko's internal profile indicated that her highest needs were for freedom and fun. With this in mind, the prospect of a future in a corporate cubicle staring at a computer screen greatly troubled her, understandably. Eventually, after some conversations with her parents and the school counselor, Tamiko changed her plans, deciding to attend a 4-year college and major in recreation management, a field much more compatible with her internal profile than computer programming.

The internal profile activities can help break down barriers between student cliques and even help overcome ethnic, racial, and other kinds of prejudice. It helps students think of diversity in a new way. Human beings are as diverse within as they are on the outside. In a suburban charter high school divided by rigid social cliques, I trained the entire student body on the internal profile over the course of a semester. The teachers followed up and supported the training in an advisory period, through activities and class meetings, and in their regular classrooms by connecting the SEL content to the curriculum. The following spring, I was happy to see when I walked through the school that students from the old cliques—the emos, the nerds, the jocks, and so forth—were talking, eating lunch, and just hanging out together. The principal told me that this year was his best ever at the school and that all the "drama" (interclique conflict) that used to take up too much of his time had all but disappeared.

In another highly multicultural urban school, one young black male student had an epiphany during a class meeting I was facilitating on the sensitive subject of racial, ethnic, and internal diversity: "You know, when we did that poster activity, I realized that I had more in common with this kid from the Czech Republic than I do with some of my boys." This young man had touched on an important point: that beneath the skin and in spite of our cultural differences, we share a common humanity that activities and conversations like these can illuminate.

Besides the benefits for students described here, an understanding of the internal profile can assist teachers in their daily interactions with students. First, understanding an individual student's internal profile can assist in differentiating instruction. For example, a student with a high love and belonging need may respond to collaborative or cooperative learning structures, whereas a student with a high freedom need may not. Instead, that student might prefer individualized learning centers or working alone on a computer. Students with a high power need might enjoy being assigned to teach the class part of a lesson in a jigsaw activity. Students with a high survival need really want clear expectations, such as a daily agenda and clear modeling and exemplars. And students with a high fun need respond to learning games and kinesthetic learning.

Similarly, a whole class of students may lean more strongly toward one need than another. In that case, it would benefit both the students and the teacher to instruct in ways that appeal to that need. More frequently, however, classes are made up of students with a variety of internal profiles, which provides another rationale for differentiating instruction. If you plan lessons and units that will appeal to all the needs, every student will be able to meet his or her individual needs at some point during the lesson or unit.

Understanding individual and class internal profiles can also help with behavior management. Students with a high survival need respond to clear behavioral expectations, consistent discipline, and the sense of order that effective procedures and routines provide. When students with a high love and belonging need break the rules, they first need to be assured that their teacher still cares about them. It's important to focus on the *behavior* as the problem, not the student personally. Students with a high power need want to be listened to. They will accept a consequence much more easily if they feel they have had a chance to be heard. Kids with a high freedom need require some choices (even if extremely limited), and students with a high fun need respond to humor when being managed.

The internal profile has powerful implications, influencing everything from how we enjoy spending our free time to the quality of our relationships to our career choices to our learning preferences to the way we perceive our world. In the next chapter, we will examine the concept of perceptions and the impact our perceptions can make on our lives.

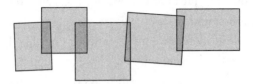

# 5 | A WORLD OF PERCEPTIONS

Many human problems stem from a lack of understanding and the indifference, fear, intolerance, anger, resentment, prejudice, bigotry, and hatred that a lack of understanding can spawn. These abstractions often manifest themselves in very tangible conflicts. In schools, students and teachers experience conflict every day, which negatively affects the climate and culture of the school, and subsequently student engagement, learning, and productivity. These conflicts not only detract from the learning environment but also add to the fear, distress, and frustration many students associate with school in general.

The first step toward reducing these kinds of problems, in school and in the world, is to increase understanding. Through helping students gain insight into (1) how we form our perceptions of the world around us and (2) the role perceptions play in our lives, we can begin to address problems born out of misunderstanding both at home and in school.

Students' perceptions of themselves, other students, school, teachers, and individual subjects are critical to their success or failure. I remember one 11th grade boy whose perception of himself as a poor English student almost held him back. I would announce close to the beginning of the semester that there would be six writing assignments that would receive credit only when students achieved a grade of *B-* or better. Students would receive specific feedback on their writing and be allowed to revise it until we—the student, the rubric, and I—agreed that it had achieved competence. The first year I made this announcement, Josh blurted, "Then I might as well quit school now. I've never gotten higher than a *C-* in my life." I smiled and said, "Congratulations!

This semester, you will." He looked at me like I had a third eye. When the bell rang, I asked him to stay after class.

I told him, "Josh, don't give up so easily. It's not like I'm going to leave you out there to do this by yourself. You'll have my support. I won't write your papers for you, but I will give you specific ways you can improve them and conference with you, if you need."

He looked at me skeptically. "Look, Mr. Erwin, that sounds good and everything, but I'm just a s--tty writer."

"So was Hemingway when he first started." (I don't know this to be true, but it sounded good at the time.) I told him, "On Thursday, I'm going to assign the first essay. If you come up to my room during activities period, I'll help you get started." He agreed.

To make a long story short, he did come up. I helped him brainstorm a topic and figure out an organizational method that would work for him. On his first version of his "final draft," Josh got a *C*-. He was pretty discouraged, but I met with him and went over my comments so he understood what to do. It took him two more revisions before we could both comfortably say it was an *A*-. I asked if he wanted to revise it one more time for a solid *A*. He declined. But his younger sister told me that his paper went up on the family refrigerator! His next paper needed only one revision. By the end of the semester, Josh handed in a solid *A* paper the first time. A couple of days later, he hung around after class. He told me, "I just thought I would always be a bad writer. Maybe I can go to college." I told him that there was no maybe about it. He ended up going to a community college and transferring to a four-year school.

Many students have perceptions of themselves as "bad in math" or "not too good in reading," and the like. Others see themselves as bad kids. I remember one 5th grader I had in summer school saying, "I'm incorrigible. The dean of students said so." I asked him what *incorrigible* means. He said, "I guess it just means that I'm bad, and I'll always be in trouble." Unless we help students understand the power of our perceptions and, in some cases, help them change unproductive perceptions, the things these kids say can easily become self-fulfilling prophecies.

The way students perceive other students, teachers, school, and specific subjects can have just as significant an impact on their future. As educators, we can teach students to be aware of perceptions and the impact they have on our behavior, and we can give them experiences that challenge their negative perceptions. We can engage in team-building activities to help break down barriers between students and help them develop positive perceptions of other students who look, sound, dress, and act differently than they do.

Teachers can improve students' perception of them by letting students get to know them as human beings, treating students fairly, and modeling respect. We can improve students' perceptions of school and our classrooms by creating a needs-satisfying environment in which students feel physically and emotionally safe (survival), are connected to adults in the school as well as other students (love and belonging), have a voice in the school or classroom (power), feel they will have the support they need to be successful (power), have choices and novel experiences (freedom), and have a chance to be playful and laugh (fun).

This chapter offers activity-based strategies aimed at helping students better understand their own perceptions and those of others.

## Teaching Students About Perceptions

CHARACTER OBJECTIVES: Students will gain information that will help develop personal and social responsibility, respect, optimism, tolerance, and acceptance.

SEL OBJECTIVES: Students will gain information that will help develop self-awareness, awareness of others, the ability to take others' perspectives, empathy, and self-evaluation skills.

PERFORMANCE OBJECTIVES: Students will demonstrate verbally or in writing an understanding that

- There is a difference between reality and perception.
- Human beings' attitudes, thoughts, and behaviors are based not on what is real but what they perceive to be real.
- Perceptions are formed (and changed) based on experience.
- Each person's "perceived world" is unique and dynamic.
- We have the ability to manage many of our perceptions.

The concept of perceptions fascinates students, and all the activities described in this chapter engage them. You may find that one activity is enough to meet your objectives, or you may want to use all of them. Teaching the concept of perceptions provides students with information they can put to use immediately in their lives, provides teachers with a new and effective approach to communicating with students, and easily connects to academic content. I invite you to try the activities in this chapter, modify them if necessary to meet your needs, but most importantly, have fun with them.

## Teaching Strategies

### *Perceptions Traffic Light*

This activity, popular among students and adults, is fun and engaging and teaches (or reminds us of) many important points about our perceptions and how they affect our behavior.

MATERIALS

- Three 6- to 8-inch-diameter circles made of construction paper (laminated): one green, one yellow, and one red

- Pictures and words cut out of magazines (matted on construction paper and laminated) and placed in large envelopes—two to three pictures or words per envelope (you might employ the students in cutting the words or pictures out of magazines they bring from home; you also might need to discuss what kinds of pictures are inappropriate for this activity)

THE ACTIVITY

1. Have the students stand or sit in a circle. Next, place the green, yellow, and red circles on the floor about 4–5 feet apart, green at the top, then yellow, then red, like a traffic light. Give each student one envelope, saying, "Please don't open this until I ask you to."

2. Explain the meanings of the colored circles: green, positive feelings; yellow, neutral feelings; and red, negative feelings.

3. Tell the class that when you say "Go," they are to open the envelopes and place each item next to the circle that best describes their first response to it. Model this for them, explaining why you are

choosing to place the items where you do. Explain that it is important not to influence where people put their items. Have them place their items where they believe they belong (without covering up one another's pictures) and return to the circle.

4. Next, start with a volunteer and then go around the circle, asking students to explain why they put their items where they did. Explain that it is important to listen to one another's reasons for putting the items in the positive, negative, or neutral space.

5. After all the students have shared their answers, ask the students if they would have put any of the pictures in a different place. If they would, ask them to choose one item that was *not* in their envelope and explain why they chose to move it. Again, go around the circle and ask all the students who moved items to share.

6. Then, pick out one of the pictures next to the green (good feelings) circle and give some really negative information about it. For example, if the picture is of a delicious-looking meal, say something like, "While this meal looks tasty, it is tainted with salmonella." Then ask the person who placed the picture near the yellow circle if, based on the new information he just heard, he would like to move it. Do the same with one of the red (bad feelings) pictures. This time give some really positive information about it. For example, someone may have put a picture with a person in it in the negative space for some reason. Say, "This person has developed a cure for cancer. Would you still put it near the red circle?"

7. Ask the students if they could find a way to change their feelings about one of the items they had in their envelopes by choosing to think differently about it. Go around the circle, inviting those who were successful in changing their feelings to share how they changed their thinking.

8. Ask the students to place any three items in their envelopes, not necessarily the original three. Ask for a volunteer to collect them, and have the rest of the class return to their seats.

## The Discussion

This postactivity discussion is where significant learning takes place. Divide the class into groups of three or four, assign a recorder for each group, and have them discuss and write down their responses to all or some of the following questions:

- What are perceptions?
- Where do our perceptions come from?
- What kinds of things affect our perceptions?
- How do our perceptions change?
- Do we have control over our perceptions?
- What effect do our perceptions have on our behavior? On our relationships?
- What else can we say about perceptions?

After 5–10 minutes of small-group discussion, hold a class meeting (see Chapter 2) about how they answered these questions. Many thoughts and insights will result from this discussion; among them might be the following:

- A perception is the way someone sees and thinks about something.
- Perceptions are based on our life experiences, including our culture, our gender, our age, where we live, how we were raised, the media, real-world events, our peers, our religious practices, and many more. Some-one may even bring up the internal profile discussed in Chapter 4. For example, it is highly likely that a person with a high freedom need will perceive things differently from a person with a high love and belonging need.
- To some extent, we can control how we perceive things. For example, we can focus on the negative aspects of something or choose to look at the positive. We can choose to be open-minded to a new experience or to resist it. Either way, our choices affect our life experience and sub-sequently our perceptions. One's world of perception, then, is in some ways chosen.
- Most, if not all, of our attitudes and behaviors are based on our perceptions.

- A person's world of perceptions is subjective, unique, constantly changing (as our experience changes), changeable, and often inaccurate or incomplete.
- For each of us, perception *is* reality.

To challenge the class's thinking about the power of perceptions, discuss how understanding the concept of perceptions can help us personally in our day-to-day lives. How about our relationships—at home and at school? Answers may include the following:

- We can choose to be optimistic or pessimistic, to look on the bright side or focus on the negative, to be happy or miserable.
- Similarly, we can choose to be open-minded or close-minded, accepting or intolerant.
- Communicating clearly and seeking accurate information are essential to avoiding misperceptions.
- Understanding the concept of perceptions can help us get along better; we'll understand others more.
- Understanding perceptions can lead to a more tolerant, more peaceful school (or community or world).

### Class Meeting on Perceptions and Stereotypes

If you believe your class has developed a certain level of trust and the students are developmentally ready, you might use the topic of perceptions as a springboard into a discussion about stereotypes of race, ethnicity, gender, age, and so forth. Following are questions and prompts for use in this version of the class meeting activity.

Step 1: Defining

1. Let's quickly review the term *perception*. Can someone please define *perception* in their own words?
2. Our class meeting topic today is stereotypes. A stereotype is a certain kind of perception. Someone, take a shot at defining *stereotype*. (If no students can provide a workable definition, give it to them: *Merriam-Webster* defines a *stereotype* as "a standardized mental

picture that is held in common by a group and that represents an oversimplified opinion [or] prejudiced attitude" (1996, p. 1153).

3. What groups of people are stereotyped? (Students will list races, ethnicities, and possibly age. You might suggest that other groups have stereotypes: men, women, gay people, the elderly, and people with various labels: learning disabled, emotional disorder, obsessive-compulsive, ADD, ADHD, Asperger's, Tourette's, and many more. After giving a few more examples, they might also list other group stereotypes that they can relate to: tweens, teenagers, preppies, emos, goths, hip-hoppers, country music lovers, metalheads, freshmen, teachers, etc.)

STEP 2: PERSONALIZING

1. What do you think are the most commonly held stereotypes in our school? (List them on the board.)

2. Have you ever been a victim of stereotyping? Let me give you my experience. We are all members of more than one group; for example, in my life, I have fit into several different categories: middle-aged, man, Scots-Irish heritage, white, English teacher, musician. So without my knowing it (or sometimes with my knowing it), I may have been thought of as (a) set in my ways because I'm middle-aged, (b) insensitive because I'm a man, (c) a cheapskate because I'm Scots-Irish, (d) unable to jump or dance because I'm white, (e) strict and rigid because I'm an English teacher, and (f) irresponsible because I was a professional musician. (Of course, you will have to list the groups you are a part of and some of the stereotypes associated with those groups.) I, personally, don't believe I have any of those characteristics, except maybe the dancing issue. You'd have to ask my wife.

3. Have any of you been aware of being stereotyped, or do you know anyone who has been stereotyped? How did it feel? Or how do you think it felt? Why did you feel that way? Or why do you think that person felt that way?

STEP 3: CHALLENGING

1. Are stereotypes true or accurate? Give an example of a false stereotype with support for your example.

2. Where do stereotypes come from? Again, provide an example.

3. Why do you think people hold stereotypes?

4. Are stereotypes generally helpful or harmful? Why?

5. How do you avoid stereotyping people?

6. If the most effective way of changing a perception is by gaining new information, what would need to happen for people to reduce or get rid of stereotypes?

This discussion should increase students' awareness of and sensitivity to issues of racial, gender, ethnic, language, and other kinds of diversity. It also gives all students the opportunity to express what it is like to be a victim of stereotyping. Listening to their classmates' stories will help students develop their ability to take others' perspective, which is one of the first steps toward developing empathy.

### Perplexing Preferences

This structured discussion is about something that interests all students: food. This once again brings out how diverse our worlds of perceptions are, even at a very basic level, like our sense of taste.

OBJECTIVE

Students will demonstrate an understanding of the following:

- Even on the most basic level, the level of the senses, our perceptions of the world differ significantly.

- Our perceptions are affected by our experience: our culture, our family, our exposure to different things, and much more.

- Our tastes (our perceptions) often change with maturity, new experiences, and so forth.

- In order for a perception to change, we must be open to the possibility.

## THE ACTIVITY

In a class meeting format, ask students to think of the following:

1. A food (or combination of foods) that they like but that many people, if not most, do not like. I give students an example by telling them that I like Brussels sprouts, an announcement that is almost always followed by groans and expressions like "Gross!"

2. A food (or combination) that they do *not* like but that many people, if not most, do. Here, I give them my example: I like chocolate and I like peanut butter, but I don't like them together. I don't like, for example, chocolate–peanut butter cups. Again, this is met with gasps of disbelief by many.

3. A change in tastes: a food (or combination) that they used to like but that they don't like anymore, or a food that they used to *not* like but that now they do like. Here, I give my examples: I used to like sweet breakfast cereals, now I prefer oatmeal with raisins only. I did not like Chinese food when I was a kid, but now I love it.

To give students a moment to think out loud about their answers in order to be ready for a large-group discussion, I have them turn to a partner and discuss their possible responses.

Next, I'll ask a volunteer to start, and quickly going around the class simply have students state their answers to question 1, then question 2, and finally question 3. It's amusing to hear the different likes, dislikes, and changes in taste.

## THE DISCUSSION

Next, divide the students into groups of three or four and assign a recorder. Explain that our taste in food is simply one kind of perception, that our perceptions are simply the way we taste, smell, hear, feel, and see the world. Ask them, "What general statements can we make about perceptions based on our food discussion?"

After giving them a few minutes to discuss in small groups, hold a large-group discussion, asking the small groups to share their answers. Here are some typical responses:

- We all have different perceptions.

- Our tastes (perceptions) are based on what we've grown up with—what we've experienced and have been taught.

- Some perceptions are better for us than others.

- Other people can influence our perceptions.

- Our perceptions often change as we get older.

- There is no right or wrong about our tastes; they are just different. This includes our tastes not only in food but also in art, music, recreational activities, and other areas.

## Curriculum Connections

As you were reading the perceptions and stereotypes activities, you probably couldn't help thinking of some ways you might integrate the concept of perceptions into the curriculum. Here are some ways teachers can make connections between these activities and the content they teach.

### English and Language Arts

JOURNALING: To encourage your students to truly integrate what they've learned about their world of perceptions, ask them to complete a series of journal entries. Daily journaling alone helps students become better writers, and some of their journal responses could be developed, through the writing process, into narratives or compositions. After the Perceptions Traffic Light or Perplexing Preferences activity, you might give students the following prompts:

- What are some of the experiences in your life that you believe have strongly influenced your perceptions of the world? Explain.

- Have you ever held a perception that you later realized was really a misperception? Tell the story.

- Have you ever changed a perception once you learned more about someone or something?

- How might you use what you've learned about perceptions to get along better with people?

- Are there any perceptions you currently hold about certain people or things that you might want to change? Why and how?

- Ask students to look at a particular current event (school related, local, or global) from multiple perspectives. For example: How do you perceive students in our school responding to the new school dress code? How might parents be responding? How about local politicians? What about a new student coming from a school that required uniforms?

After the Perplexing Preferences activity, you might prompt students to answer the following questions:

- Besides your tastes, what other perceptions have changed as you've gotten older?

- Are there some foods you like that are not good for you? Are there any other perceptions (ways of looking at people, places, and things) you have that are not necessarily helpful for you to hold? Discuss.

- Are you open to trying new foods? Are you open to changing other perceptions? Explain.

POINT OF VIEW IN LITERATURE: Another logical connection to the English or language arts curriculum is to examine point of view in literature. Students will gain an appreciation for how the storyteller's perceptions or perspective can have a profound effect on the meaning of the story and the way the story is interpreted by the reader/listener. They will also understand that we must take into account the point of view from which a story is told in assessing the story's meaning and accuracy.

Read or tell a well-known story from a perspective that puts a different spin on the traditional tale. You might choose to tell one of the following stories:

- *Hansel and Gretel* from the witch's perspective (maybe she wasn't a witch)

- *Jack and the Beanstalk* from the Giant's point of view or from that of Jack's mother

- *Snow White* from one of the dwarves' perspectives or maybe from a couple different dwarves' perspectives (Happy's version of events may differ significantly from Grumpy's)

You could have a lot of fun coming up with a new version of a traditional tale. If you don't have the inclination or time to rewrite a classic, you could use one that already exists. For example, *The Real Story of the Three Little Pigs* (Scieszka & Smith, 1996), a hit with both kids and adults, tells the traditional story of the three pigs from the Big, Bad Wolf's point of view. (He wasn't so big and bad after all.) Another well-known literary experiment with point of view is John Gardner's (1985) *Grendel*, which tells the *Beowulf* legend from the monster's perspective. (*Caution*: While *Grendel* is one of my personal favorites, it contains language that some parents may find questionable. My defense: What kind of language *would* a monster use? I taught this novel to my senior English students, sending a letter home to parents warning them and explaining that an alternate novel could be assigned for their child if they had objections.) You may be aware of other literature that uses the same technique of experimenting with point of view.

After reading the story or excerpt, hold a class meeting on the impact of the perceptions of the storyteller on the narrative. You might bring up or ask for situations in the students' lives where the perspective of the storyteller influences the story. For example, two students in an argument or fight might tell different versions of events. A teacher and a student may tell different stories about why the student is serving detention. They will surely have experiences they would like to relate.

Next, you might assign the students to write a well-known story from a different point of view. First, on the board, brainstorm a list of stories that most students know. Take one or two of the stories, and examine the different points of view from which that same story might be told. Have them pick one and use the writing process to develop a final writing product. When they complete their new versions of old stories, have the students share them with the class.

### Social Studies

Point of View in History: Instead of using fiction, focus on historical events as the way of examining point of view. You might provide an example from U.S. history like the Boston Tea Party. How might the same event be described by one of the participants, by a Boston Loyalist, or by a Native American? If possible, show students texts that provide differing points of view on historical events. Then brainstorm some historical events that they might use to experiment with perspective. Assign them to pairs or small groups and ask them to write letters to the editor or articles for a history book that describe that event from as many perspectives as there are students in the group. Then have each group share the varying perspectives and discuss why each person would look at the event in the way he or she does.

POINT OF VIEW IN CURRENT EVENTS: Have students analyze and discuss current events from different perspectives. Read a news article, a sports article, or an op-ed piece to them and ask them to free-write about the issue or events from a variety of perspectives. After sharing their writing with the class, you might assign them to seek out a current event they are interested in, research it from different perspectives, and write about it from two or three points of view. For example, a student might choose to write a reaction to Hurricane Katrina, which devastated New Orleans in 2005, from the point of view of a survivor, a member of the National Guard involved in the rescue and relief effort, the president, or a Weather Channel reporter. Another student may choose to write about the $700 billion bailout of the banking and mortgage industry in 2008 from the point of view of a bank CEO, a member of Congress, a taxpayer, an unemployed auto worker, or President Bush or President Obama. This assignment could easily be extended to include a research paper, a panel discussion, a role-play, or a debate.

PROPAGANDA: Examine propaganda from World War II, the Korean War, or the Vietnam War from both sides (if possible), analyzing the messages that were being conveyed in the propaganda, verbally and visually, and how these messages were intended to impact the public's perceptions.

POLITICAL CARTOONS: Display political cartoons from various periods in history and today, and analyze the way the cartoonists attempt to impact the perceptions of their audience.

POLITICAL ADS: Analyze the ways opponents in a political contest try to manipulate perceptions of the voting public through the media.

NEWS: Discuss how some media corporations are considered conservative and some liberal. Compare and contrast the ways news events are reported by different newspapers, magazines, Internet news sites, or magazines.

### Business

Teach and discuss with students how advertising companies attempt to manipulate our perceptions in ways that will sell their product. You might assign students, individually or in teams, to create and present (live or on video) an advertisement for an innovative fantasy product, making sure they use one or more of the techniques they learned and observed.

### Technology

1. Discuss how the ever-increasing pace of technological development affects our perceptions of things such as the world in general, shopping, communication, dating, privacy, and so forth.

2. Students today are using social networking sites, cell phones, text messaging, e-mail, and other forms of electronic communication that involve issues related to perceptions. One topic you might discuss with them is the danger associated with Internet predators. You might have a class meeting asking questions about their experiences with chat rooms, MySpace, Facebook, e-mail, and texting. Do they always know who they are communicating with? Have they ever heard of any dangers involved? What might be the difference between who they perceive they are communicating with and reality? What are some commonsense safety tips for people and their use of these electronic media?

### Art

These activities are ones that my wife, Holly, has used in her art classrooms.

FOR UPPER ELEMENTARY AND MIDDLE SCHOOL: Give each student a manila envelope with a coloring sheet of the same famous work of art and two markers or crayons. Make sure each student's colors and kinds of markers or crayons are as different from other students' as possible: some bright colors, some warm colors, some cool, some neutrals. Some should be standard crayons, some glitter crayons, some small markers, some larger. Have the students color their sheets using only the items in their envelopes. Afterward in a class meeting, put all the colored sheets in the middle of the circle and compare how the colors and type of instrument affect the way they perceive the work of art. Ask the following questions:

- What do you notice when you look at all the colored sheets?
- (Choose two very differently colored sheets.) What kinds of thoughts or feelings do you have when you look at these two? Why? (Choose another two and do the same.)
- Do colors affect the way we think or feel? How?
- Next, show students two paintings in which the use of color and what color expresses in the two works can be starkly contrasted. Discuss as a class the different ideas and feelings the colors in the two works elicit from the students. Then you might give them your interpretation.

This class meeting might lead to an assignment to pairs or small groups of students to be assigned two works of art, to compare and contrast the artists' use of color in them, and to make a presentation to the class.

FOR MIDDLE AND HIGH SCHOOL: Display three still-life paintings by artists from different periods or different styles. Then ask:

- In what ways are these paintings similar?
- What differences do you notice?
- What do you think the differences might tell us about the perceptions of the different artists or the times and places in which they lived?

## Music

Play a variety of (mostly instrumental) selections and have students number their papers and write down the thoughts or feelings for each of these selections. You might choose to play one of these pieces:

- The end of Handel's *Messiah*
- Tiny Tim's "Tiptoe Through the Tulips"
- Anything by Miles Davis
- The end of Tchaikovsky's *1812 Overture*
- "Pick Up the Pieces" by Average White Band
- The theme from *Rocky*

After you play each selection, with time in between for the students to take notes, hold a class meeting, playing a small part of each piece. Discuss the following questions:

- What kind of music would you say this is (let them know if they don't).
- What thoughts or feelings did this piece create for you?
- Why? What aspect of the music (the rhythm, volume, tempo, melody, etc.) created that feeling or those thoughts for you?
- Do any of the selections seem to have the same effect on most people? Why?
- Could someone use music to manipulate another person? Who? How? (Examples might be relaxing music in dentists' offices, music in films, commercials, etc.)

You might assign students to work in pairs or small groups and compare and contrast music from a particular artist, genre, or period. Or they might compare and contrast music from different genres that inspires similar feelings. Have them present their music and report their analysis to the class.

## Conclusion

Understanding the concept of perception can benefit both teachers and students. Leading students through these activities and discussions reminds teachers of the importance of students' perceptions of themselves and their own abilities, the subject, and the teacher in determining their success. It also reminds us of the importance of providing clear expectations for students. It is helpful for teachers to clearly explain, discuss, and check for understanding of points like these:

- How students will be expected to behave and why
- What the students' responsibilities are and are not
- What they can and cannot expect from the teacher
- What they will be asked to learn and why
- How they will be assessed

These goals can be accomplished through a variety of means, including activities such as the Class Constitution, My Job/Your Job, and class meetings (see Erwin, 2004). One thing is clear: if the teacher's expectations are vague, there may well be as many different interpretations of the rules and learning objectives as there are students in the class.

Everyone in the class can benefit from an awareness of the fact that there are as many ways of seeing the world as there are individuals. Understanding this concept can empower us to challenge the perceptions that we hold, become open to seeing things from a different perspective, reject stereotypes and bigotry as misperceptions, and gain a better understanding of ourselves and others. Understanding leads to tolerance, then acceptance, empathy, and eventually compassion. A clearer way of seeing the world can lead us to a better way of being a part of the classroom, the school, and the world.

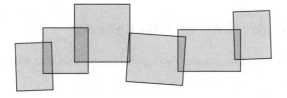

# 6 | THE CONCEPT OF TOTAL BEHAVIOR, OR DRIVING YOUR BEHAVIORAL CAR

*True strength is not the ability to control others;*
*it is the ability to control oneself.*

—Hideo Ochiai, member of the
Black Belt Hall of Fame

Almost everyone has heard or used an expression like "He's driving me crazy!" or "That is driving me up the wall!" It is true that people sometimes behave in ways that we find frustrating, and things in our lives are frequently not the way we'd like them to be. However, we still always have a choice over how we respond to them. We can allow our environment to *drive* us. Or we can take effective control over our response to the frustrations we encounter in our daily lives.

This chapter explains how to teach students a powerful concept in helping them learn to self-regulate, how to "drive themselves" effectively and responsibly—the concept of *total behavior* (Glasser, 1986). Although the concept is profound, it can be taught through a simple, concrete metaphor, one to which any student can easily relate: the automobile. I will be referring to it as the behavioral car. The following process is one I have used hundreds of times to teach students, from 3rd graders through adults, about their behavioral car. Students stop perceiving themselves as victims of their environment and instead see themselves as purposeful, active, driving forces in their own lives.

## Teaching Students About Total Behavior

CHARACTER OBJECTIVES: Students will gain information that will help develop personal responsibility and self-control.

SEL OBJECTIVES: Students will gain information that will help develop the skills of self-awareness, metacognition, emotion identification, self-regulation, impulse control, and anger and stress management.

PERFORMANCE OBJECTIVES: Students will demonstrate an understanding of the following:

- There are four components to total behavior: actions, thoughts, feelings, and physiology.
- All four components of total behavior are always present.
- The change in any one component affects the other three.
- We have direct control over our actions and thoughts, but we can only indirectly control our feelings and (to a lesser extent) our physiology.
- We are in most effective (and responsible) control when we are driven by "front wheel" behavior (actions and thoughts) rather than "back wheel" behavior (feelings and physiology).
- We can choose to allow others to influence the various components of our total behavior, but ultimately, we are in control.

The activities in this chapter are carefully sequenced to help students understand the concepts, then personalize them, and finally gain the skills to apply them to their lives. They don't all have to be done within the same day or even the same week, but they are designed to be carried out in the order they appear.

### Teaching Strategies

#### Minilecture

First, students need to understand the concept of *total behavior* and its four components: actions, thoughts, feelings, and physiology. I show the class an overhead with the concept of total behavior and the four components defined (Figure 6.1).

Next, I explain total behavior to students as follows (you will want to use your own examples):

## Total Behavior

Normally, when we think of behavior, we think of actions, what someone is doing. *Total behavior*, however, is more than just what people are doing; it also includes their thoughts, feelings, and physiology. All four of these components of total behavior are present all the time and change from moment to moment. We are often more aware of one component than others, but every total behavior includes all four.

For example, if I am running, the most obvious component is the actions component. However, while I am running, I may be thinking, "What a beautiful spring morning!" Along with that action and thought, I may feel a sense of well-being and exhilaration. The physiological component would include elevated heart and breathing rates, sweating, and endorphin production. All four components would be, in this slice of time, my total behavior of running. When one component changes, the other three change as well. If, for example, my thought changes from "What a beautiful spring morning!" to "Oh, no, here comes that ill-tempered pit bull," my actions, feelings, and physiology will change accordingly. My eight-minute-per-mile pace may change to a sprint, my feelings may change from well-being to fear, and my adrenal gland may shift into high gear.

If I am meditating, the most prominent component of total behavior is the thoughts component. I am focusing on a single thought or an image. Although there is little action, I am still doing something: I'm sitting.

---

**6.1  Total Behavior**

All behavior is made up of four components: **actions, thoughts, feelings,** and **physiology**.

**ACTIONS**: what we are doing

**THOUGHTS**: the stream of thoughts constantly running through our minds

**FEELINGS**: our emotions (anger, fear, joy, etc.)

**PHYSIOLOGY** (or body talk): all our nonconscious physical responses (e.g., heart rate, breathing, sweating, muscle tension, hormone levels, brain chemistry, etc.)

Calm and peacefulness are the dominant feelings, and my physiology slows down; my heart rate decreases, and my breathing is slow and deep. This is the total behavior of meditation.

If feelings, or emotion, is the most apparent component—for example, if I am extremely angry—the other components are present as well. Physically, I may be tense and flushed. My brain chemistry is affected, and my blood pressure may become elevated. I might be thinking something like "I can't believe he said that!" And my actions may include pacing back and forth and venting to anyone who will listen. While all four components of my total behavior are affected, in this case I am most aware of my feelings. Finally, if I am sick to my stomach, the most prominent component of total behavior is physiology—my nausea has my full attention. My thinking may be "Oh, please make this go away." I am probably feeling upset and sorry for myself. And my actions are to lie down and try to sleep. So, like the other examples, we name the behavior of the moment, being sick, by the most prominent component, which in this case is physiology.

### The Behavioral Car

Once students understand that behavior is made up of four components (actions, thoughts, feelings, and physiology), you can introduce the analogy of the behavioral car. Show the students a visual of a car with the four wheels labeled as in Figure 6.2. It is important that the front wheels are labeled "actions" and "thoughts" and the back wheels are labeled "feelings" and "physiology" (or "body talk" for younger students).

---

**6.2   The Four Wheels of Your Behavioral Car**

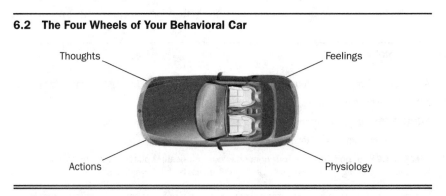

Then, ask the students, "In what ways are people like a car?" If you think they may not be ready to make the important connections, you might just tell them: Like cars, we are all heading in a direction in life; we can move forward or backward; we are constantly adjusting to stay on the road; we frequently need to make important choices (turns at intersections); if we're not careful, we can get hurt or hurt others.

If the students have learned about the five basic needs (see Chapter 3), you might go on to explain that cars have one fuel tank and need gasoline in order to run properly, but human beings have five fuel tanks: survival, love and belonging, power, freedom, and fun. These five needs fuel all of our behavior. At this point, the students have been listening long enough and need to be active.

### Think Red

This activity is an effective and enjoyable way to help students experience total behavior and learn the basics of self-regulation. Begin this activity by asking your students to stand up at their desks. Explain that they are going to be a part of an experiment with *total behavior*, that you are going to ask them to control each of the four components of total behavior they just learned about, and that their job is simply to do their best to follow your directions. Also, explain that it is important that they do this activity with their eyes closed and without talking. Once they all have their eyes closed and are quiet, give the following directions, waiting three to five seconds after each step:

1. *Thoughts*: "First, I'm going to ask you to control your thinking. Think red; try to see the color red with your mind's eye." Wait three to five seconds and then say, "Now think green; try to see the color green with your mind's eye." Again wait three to five seconds and say, "Stop thinking green."

2. *Feelings*: "Now I'm going to ask you to control your feelings. Keeping your eyes closed, try to feel angry." (Pause) "Feel sad." (Pause) "Stop feeling sad and be happy." (Pause) Giggles may follow some of the directions. There's no need to stop the activity. You may want to bring that behavior into the postactivity discussion. ("What were you *thinking* when you giggled?")

3. *Physiology*: "Next, I'm going to ask you to control your body. Again, keeping your eyes closed, raise your heart rate." (During the pause some students may start running in place. That's OK—they are simply complying with your directions.) "Lower your cholesterol." (There will be some chuckles and probably a comment such as "I need some Cheerios.") Third, ask them to "Sweat profusely. [Pause] Now stop sweating."

4. *Actions*: "Now, I'm going to ask you to control your 'doing' behavior, your actions. First raise your right hand. [You won't need much of a pause between these directions.] Lower it. Touch your nose. Stop touching your nose. Open your eyes, and sit down, please."

Discussion

Now, using an image of the behavioral car, point to each wheel, labeled as in Figure 6.2, and review everything you asked the students to do, as follows.

1. Tell the students, "First, I asked you to think red, think green, and stop thinking green. Then I asked you to feel angry, feel sad, and stop feeling sad, and so forth."

2. Ask, "Of all four components of total behavior—actions, thoughts, feelings, and physiology—which are the easiest components to control?" Invariably, the students will say, "Actions" or "Thoughts." Respond, "Yes, it's really easy to raise your hand, touch your nose, and open your eyes; and it's pretty easy to think of something red or green." Go on to explain, "That's why the front two wheels are actions and thoughts. When we're driving, we turn the steering wheel, and it's the front two wheels that change direction, and the back wheels follow along."

3. Ask, "What did you do when I said stop thinking green?" The answers will vary but may include "I went back to red," "I kept thinking green," or "I thought black." The point is we never stop thinking. Whether we are aware of it or not, the thinking wheel is always spinning, even when we sleep.

4. Ask, "Was anyone able to feel angry or sad or happy when directed to?" Usually, most students raise their hands. Ask them, "How

did you do it?" and they will invariably say that they thought of someone or something that "makes" them mad or sad or happy. Respond, "Exactly! It is our thoughts that create our feelings! We form a thought in the brain's cerebral cortex. This 'thought information' becomes an electrochemical impulse that travels via the amygdala through the limbic system, the emotional center of the brain, creating a feeling. This happens in a split second, which is why we aren't aware that *we create our feelings; they don't just happen to us.*"

5. Ask, "How many of you were able to raise your heart rate?" Some students will raise their hands. "How did you manage that?" Students will respond with answers such as "I ran in place," "I held my breath," or "I thought of something that stressed me out." Point out that they once again were able to *indirectly* control a "back wheel" behavior (physiology) by directly controlling one of their front wheels, by doing or thinking something.

6. Before concluding, ask the students, "When people drive, where do they sit, in the front seat or the back?" (The front, of course.) "What would happen if people drove from the backseat?" (A student might say something like, "My dad says my mom is a backseat driver," which gets a laugh.) "I mean this literally. What would happen if we sat in the backseat and tried to drive?" The students will say, "They would crash" or "They'd go off the road." Go on and elaborate: "Exactly! But people drive their behavioral cars from the back all the time. They let their feelings or their physiology drive their front wheels." At this point I usually tell the students that I once heard someone jokingly say, "I'm in a bad mood, so I'm not responsible for anything I say or do today." This is an example of someone letting their feelings (bad mood) drive her actions and simultaneously relieve herself of any responsibility for them. The students will laugh, but most get the point.

7. Ask, "What wheel would represent anger?" They'll see that anger is a back wheel (feeling) behavior. "What would happen if someone lets anger drive his behavioral car?" It's easy for students to come

up with examples of ineffective and irresponsible actions if people allowed the back wheel behavior of anger to drive their whole car.

8. At this point I'll usually tell the students that I once watched a student come into a 7th grade math class announcing, "I didn't take my medication today. Watch out for me!" In this instance, the student was using his physiology as a way of shirking his responsibility for his actions. It may well be that it is more difficult to attend in math class without his medication, but he can still control his front wheels if he has the will and the skills to do so.

9. Finally, ask the students to turn to a partner and summarize what they have learned about their behavioral cars through this activity. After a minute or two, ask them to share their conclusions with the class. They will state, among other things:

- There are four parts (wheels) of our total behavior: actions, thoughts, feelings, and physiology.
- We have the most control over our front wheels, actions and thoughts.
- We have indirect control over our feelings and physiology.
- We drive our behavior cars most effectively when we concentrate on front wheel behavior.
- It's not a good idea to try to drive our cars from the backseat. When we let our feelings or physiology drive our behavior, we often do things that are ineffective or irresponsible. In other words, we crash our cars.
- If we don't like how we're feeling (emotionally or physically), we should change what we're doing or thinking.

10. At the end of the discussion, you might issue students a key chain, to remind them that they hold the keys to their behavioral car. Give them the assignment to come in the next day with a key for their key chain, one from home that no one needs anymore. I have found that this is not a difficult assignment; most families have old keys lying around. You could pick up a few blank keys from a local

hardware store to give to students just in case they couldn't find one at home.

### The Behavioral Car Keys and Driver's License

The day after the Think Red experience and discussion, we will briefly review the concept of the behavioral car. Then I'll ask the students to take out their key chains. Next, I'll distribute a behavioral driver's license to each student saying, "Congratulations, you've all just earned your behavioral driver's license and car keys! No one can take your keys away from you. You might occasionally choose to give them away temporarily, however."

At this point, it is important to help the students make the connection between "giving away their car keys" and allowing others to control or influence what they do, think, or feel (emotionally or physically). Students in particular perceive that others are in charge a lot of the time (way too much, according to many of them). We don't want our students suddenly announcing to their parents and teachers, "You can't drive my car. You can't make me do anything!" We want them, instead, to understand that they choose to follow rules, for example. So we need to have a discussion in which we ask:

- Who do your parents give their car keys to?
- When you buy a car, who do you think you will lend your car keys to?

Almost without fail, students will answer that their parents and they themselves will only lend their car keys to relatives and close friends, if anyone—in other words, people they can trust. I make the connection for them, stating, "And that is why we often give our behavioral car keys to our parents, teachers, coaches, and other adults. We choose to listen to them, obey rules, and give them some decision-making power over us. We know that they care about us and have our best interests in mind."

Next, I'll ask, "Who should we *not* lend our behavioral car keys to?" Answers will include the following:

- People who are trying to make us angry, sad, afraid, and so forth
- People who are trying to pressure us into doing something we know is wrong or irresponsible
- People who don't care about us

- People we don't trust
- People we don't know

Next, after summarizing what we've learned about the behavioral car, I explain to the class that I will continue to refer to the car metaphor throughout the year. I tell them that I'll be like a friendly traffic cop, asking them to self-evaluate their behavior and drive their cars responsibly by asking questions like these:

- Who is driving your car?
- Did you give your car keys to _____?
- Are you driving from the back or the front seat?
- Is your car on the road or in the ditch?
- Where is your car going to end up if you keep driving it this way?
- Are you steering your car where you want to go?
- Are you looking where you are driving?

I'm sure that as you continue to use the car metaphor, you and your students will develop new questions and ways of connecting the car to behavior. Parents will appreciate learning about the car as well. One parent I recently met told me that she and her husband were having a disagreement, and her 9-year-old daughter asked her, "Did you give your car keys to Dad? Are you letting him drive your car?" Having a consistent way of discussing behavior at school and at home will help students practice self-regulation and self-efficacy, skills necessary to becoming responsible members of the community.

### The Behavioral Traffic Circle

This cooperative group activity expands on the car analogy. You begin this activity by dividing the class up into pairs or small groups, giving each group a big sheet of chart paper or newsprint. Have the students draw a traffic circle with four exits. To save time, you might want to provide them with the traffic circles yourself (see Figure 6.3). If you laminate several traffic circles, you can use them year after year. Just have the students write on them with erasable markers or transparency pens. Next, you give each group of students a scenario that students might respond to with anger or frustration. One scenario might be "Brittany just called you stupid." The pairs or groups then generate three or four different possible choices of total behavior, one for each of the exits on the traffic circle. Next to each exit the students identify the actions, thoughts, feelings, and physiology involved in each choice. For example, one behavior a student might choose to respond to Brittany would be to call her a name. Next to the first exit the students would write:

Action: Calling Brittany a jerk.
Thought: "I can't stand her. She is always so nasty."
Feeling: Angry
Physiology: Hot, sweating, tense, heart beating fast

### 6.3 Traffic Circle

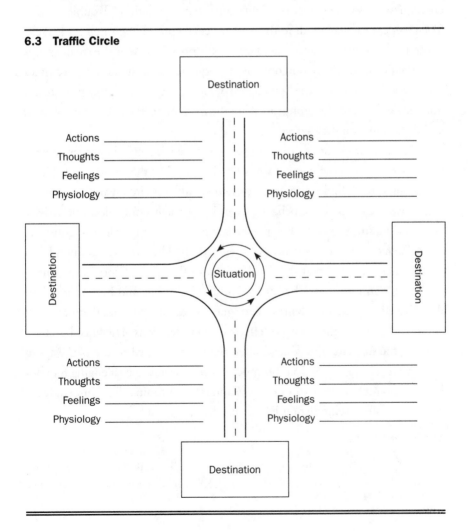

Another exit might say:

    Action: Focusing on school work, ignoring Brittany

    Thoughts: "I'm not going to let Brittany drive my car."

    Feeling: Calm

    Physiology: Cool, relaxed

After the students have generated three or four choices, ask them to identify the destination to which each total behavior might take them. In other words, what might the natural or imposed consequences of each choice, or exit, be? The first choice in our example might result in the teacher doling out consequences, so the students might name that destination "Trouble Town." The latter choice may result in the student feeling proud of himself for his self-control. Maybe the students would call this "Prideville." After the small groups have predicted the likely outcome or consequence of each choice, have them identify the exit that has the best chance of taking them where they want to go. You may even want the groups to share their scenarios, their different choices, and the destination they agreed on.

This activity teaches students in very concrete terms that in any given situation there are always choices. Even when it seems like the world is conspiring against us and we find ourselves in extremely difficult circumstances, how we behave (where we drive our behavioral car) is ultimately our choice. The activity also provides students with the opportunity to practice, in a safe way, considering deliberately the consequences of their actions. The latest research on brain development suggests that the development of the cerebral cortex, the thinking brain, continues into the early or mid-20s. Middle and high school students have just gotten the hardware, or gray matter, that enables them to think ahead and consider the results or effects of their decisions. They need practice in using the software, the white matter, the myelin-coated neural pathways in their brain. Through practice, this process, which seems so challenging for adolescents, becomes almost automatic. Without opportunities like this, students' complete brain development is left to chance.

### The Instant Tune-up

Every car, even the most finely engineered vehicle in the world, needs an occasional tune-up for optimal performance. If cars don't get the maintenance they need, if they've been driven hard or are running hot, they do things that we don't like. They run sluggishly, make strange noises, and eventually may break down completely. The parallel to students is remarkable. The human equivalent of being "driven hard" results in distress, and students sometimes "overheat" with frustration or anger. When students are feeling distressed, highly frustrated, or angry, they, like cars, do things we don't like: they stop working, disrupt class (make strange noises), and sometimes break down completely. When that happens, teachers often end up sending the student to the school's version of the automotive service center, the office, to be "repaired" by a professional, the assistant principal or a counselor. Just like taking the car to the dealer for service, sending students to the office can be costly (in time, paperwork, and damage to relationships). Another problem with sending students to the office is when they get there, they often don't exhibit the same behaviors that resulted in their being sent to the office in the first place, just like when a car stops making the strange sounds as soon as the mechanic takes it for a test drive. Then the teacher ends up wasting more time trying to convince the disciplinarian that he or she wasn't being too impatient—that it really was the student's behavior, not the teacher's, that was the problem. We can avoid a lot, if not all, of these kinds of problems by teaching students how to maintain their own behavioral cars when they are overly stressed, frustrated, or angry.

Teaching students how to tune up their own behavioral cars (i.e., manage stress and anger) may take a little time initially, but in the long run, it can save time and energy for everyone involved. It's best to teach students this when they are *not* stressed or angry, maybe as part of a behavioral car mini-unit.

Since we know that it is our thoughts that create our feelings, explain to your students that certain kinds of *trigger thoughts* create stress and anger. Having these thoughts is like stepping on the accelerator, revving up our emotional engines. Following are some different types of trigger thoughts.

STRESS

- Fear of failure ("I'll never be able to . . ." "I'm not any good at . . .")
- Fear of how others will react ("What will everyone think of me if . . . ?" "I'll look stupid (unskilled, funny, incompetent, etc.) if . . .")

- Feeling trapped ("There is no way out of this mess." "I'll never get out of here.")
- Catastrophizing ("My whole life is going to be ruined if . . ." "There goes my future.")

Invite students to think of or write in their journals about other thoughts they or others might have when they are feeling stressed out.

ANGER

- "Always" or "never" thinking ("I *never* get to . . ." "This coach is *always* on my case." "No one *ever* listens to me.")
- Labeling ("That person is a complete jerk!" "This class is such a waste of time!")
- Fairness issues ("This is so unfair." "I always get the shaft.")

Again, you might ask students to write about some other thoughts they or others might have when they first become angry. These thoughts that come early in our anger episodes only serve to water the seeds of our anger, increasing its intensity and prolonging its duration. It is while we are having these initial thoughts that we can take control and transform our anger. Some students might list other thoughts that occur after these first thoughts have fueled our anger to the point that we are seeking release from the tension of anger. These thoughts are often violent, destructive, or self-destructive. It is much harder to manage our anger when it has gotten to this point. It is more effective to focus our energy on transforming those initial trigger thoughts.

It is not a good idea to try to directly resist anger. That would be like trying to hold back a stampeding mob. Instead, we want students to recognize their anger and take care of it, as one would take care of a small child who has lost her way home. As we might gently guide a child until she is in the arms of her parents, we can gently guide our anger until we are in an emotionally safer place.

To take effective control of our anger and to not let it drive our behavioral car in a direction we may later regret, we only need to remember three simple steps: (1) turn off the ignition, (2) relax, and (3) restart.

1. TURN OFF THE IGNITION. The first step in the process is to stop the thoughts that are creating or increasing our anger or stress. We can effectively interrupt our thoughts and turn off the ignition of an angry or stressed behavioral car by

deliberately using tough self-talk, saying (maybe shouting) to ourselves (silently, of course) words, phrases, or imperatives like these:

- Stop it!
- Knock it off!
- What are you *doing*?!
- Time out!
- Take a chill pill!
- Whoa!

2. RELAX (AND BREATHE): Once we have interrupted our stress or anger, the next thing to do is to relax ourselves physically. It is easy to maintain or increase our anger or stress if our bodies are hot and tense. It is important, therefore, to identify our physical signals and to learn how to breathe properly.

Our physical signals are like the warning lights on the dashboard of our cars. Ask students to identify where in their bodies they feel tension when they are stressed or angry. Do their shoulders tighten up, or do they feel tension in their jaws? A student's hot spot might be in her forehead, neck, abdomen, or legs. Once students have identified their warning lights, ask them to pick two or three coping, thinking, and breathing strategies that can help them relax. They might choose from the following self-talk statements or make up their own:

- Take a deep breath and relax.
- Breathe and relax the hot spots.
- Breathe the stress/anger away.
- It's time to breathe and calm down.
- Shrug and relax the shoulders.
- Check body for tension, and relax what's tight.

It's also important for students to learn how to breathe correctly. Shallow or chest breathing does little or nothing to relax tension. Deep, abdominal breathing, or breathing with the diaphragm, is what works. Have students practice by placing one hand on their abdomen and the other on their chest. When they take a deep breath, their stomachs should expand before their chests. Have them practice this natural breathing a few times so that they can do it automatically.

3. RESTART: Once we have interrupted the kind of thinking that increases our stress or anger and have begun relaxing those hot spots and taken a few deep breaths, we can now take more effective control over our feelings by replacing those volatile thoughts with more rational, calming self-talk. Ask students to choose (or modify) a couple of the following statements that they think will help them remain calm and feel in control:

- It's not worth it to lose my temper (or to stress out).
- In 100 years (or five years, or a month), who will know the difference?
- Who is driving my car right now? Is that what I want?
- Get in the front seat.
- Don't sweat the small stuff.
- Getting stressed (or angry) will cost me _____.
- Getting upset won't help.
- I'm annoyed, but I can stay calm.
- Keep your voice calm and cool.
- Strong people control themselves.
- Don't escalate. Chill.
- No matter what they say, I know I'm a good (strong, smart) person.
- I can stay in control.
- It's going to be OK.
- Isn't it interesting how this person is trying to make me angry (afraid, feel bad)?
- I'm not going to let him (this situation) get the best of me.
- Losing it only gives him what he wants.
- Stressing (or getting angry) isn't going to help anything. Stay cool.

In order for this three-step process to become automatic, students need practice. You might give each student an index card. At the top, have them identify an action or statement that in the past has provoked stress or anger. Then direct the class to write down the three-step Instant Tune-up process, including the specific thoughts and actions the students will use to turn off the ignition, relax (including the specific hot spots), and restart. Next, pair students up and have them practice their process. One student might say or do what her partner has identified as something that has provoked her in the past. The other student would then say aloud the thoughts and practice the relaxation strategies he has determined will help. Then students would switch roles. The teacher might then have students switch partners and repeat the process. The teacher may even have students use their index card as a bookmark or tape it to their desk or locker for a few weeks as a continual reminder.

I have used the Tune-up technique with students as old as 12th graders and with children as young as my own 7-year-old stepson Liam, my son Nate when he was 3, and my 2-year-old daughter Laena. Once during a class meeting, some of my seniors complained about how stressed they get over unit tests, midterms, and final exams. I asked if they would like to learn a relaxation technique, and they responded with an enthusiastic "Yes!" So the next day, I played some soothing music, asked them to get into a comfortable position, and led them through a guided relaxation and breathing activity, having them focus on relaxing their bodies on the inhalation and repeating a positive thought (one they came up with) silently to themselves on the exhalation. Some complained that "This isn't yoga class" (but did the exercise anyway), but most students really seemed to enjoy it. One student, Nicelle, told me privately later on that she had been experiencing what she thought were panic attacks in school, and since she started doing the Tune-up two or three times a day, she wasn't experiencing them anymore.

When my own children become agitated, we encourage them to "calm themselves down," which means to give themselves a tune-up. In the case of 2-year-old Laena, when she starts to tantrum, I escort her to the "big chair" and encourage her to take three deep breaths. She immediately starts to calm down. If I stop then, she starts winding back up again, so I continue to have her breathe (modeling it as she goes) and ask her to say, "Mommy and Daddy love me" as she exhales. Within five minutes, she is calm and ready to rejoin the family.

### The Trade-in

Controlling ourselves in the heat of the moment is not easy, but being proactive and having a simple process like the Instant Tune-up can make it manageable. A few years ago, I taught a group of high school students about the concept of the behavioral car. The very next morning, one of the boys in the group, a senior named Zach, hurried up to me, saying, "Mr. Erwin, this stuff really works!" I asked him to tell me more. He explained that the previous afternoon, just as school got out, he and his girlfriend had an argument. He said he was so angry that when he got to his car in the school parking lot, he was "gonna tear out of that parking lot and down the road and . . . didn't care who was in the way." He went on: "Then I had this thought, 'Who's driving my car?' It just took a nanosecond, and I was able to get back in control. I took a couple deep breaths and decided fighting with her wasn't worth killing someone over. So I just took a ride instead of going berserk. Cool, huh?" And then he went to homeroom.

As "cool" as it is to be able to have the coping skills that enable you to tune your behavioral car up in a "nanosecond," it might be better not to drive that stressed or hot car at all. In other words, if repairs on your old car are becoming too frequent or too costly, there is a time to cut your losses and trade it in for something more reliable, a better-performing vehicle. The process involved in the Trade-in is based on a process originally titled Reinventing Yourself (Boffey, 1993). But like going to a car dealer, negotiating a trade-in, and buying a new car, this process takes time, planning, and rational thinking. So it is vital to wait for the right time to undergo this process, a time when the person involved is calm and able to think clearly, not when he is emotionally charged up.

Steps

1. The first step in this process involves analyzing the behavior the student wants to replace. Ask students to think of a situation they commonly experience in which they drive a behavioral car that isn't working very well for them. For example, there might be a place such as the bus, the cafeteria, or a particular class where they regularly feel stressed or angry and then act out their stress or anger, ending up in trouble or feeling worse. Or there might be a person (a sibling, a bully, maybe even a teacher) who "pushes their buttons," or a task (taking out the trash, performing a writing assignment, or participating in physical education) they have an aversion to. I model what I'm asking them to do on the board using an appropriate personal example (working for a bullying boss I once had before I went into teaching).

2. Once they have identified a recurring stressful situation, starting with the back wheels, ask the students to name the feelings they want to transform (annoyance, frustration, anger, stress, etc.) and to write the feeling(s) in the appropriate quadrant of the Trade-in worksheet (see Figure 6.4).

3. The next step is to identify and write down the accompanying physical response in the physiology quadrant. If the feeling is anger, for example, the physiology might include tensing muscles, feeling hot, or shaking.

4. Next, have students try to identify and write down the kinds of thoughts they have in that situation that serve to sustain or increase their negative feelings. You might refer back to the stressful

**6.4  Trade-in**

| Actions | Thoughts |
|---------|----------|
|         |          |
| Feelings | Physiology |
|         |          |

thoughts (fear of failure, catastrophizing, etc.) or angry thoughts (always or never thinking, fairness issues) listed earlier to help them.

5. Now have them write the actions they choose that they later regret. Once they have completed their Trade-in worksheet, ask them to give this behavioral car a name. I might call mine Stressed-out Sedan, Rage Rover, or Jon's Junker to give them some ideas. Have them set that worksheet aside and tell them, "We're trading in that behavioral car for a new model."

6. Next, ask them to go to the New Behavioral Car worksheet (see Figure 6.5). Explain that we can't control the person or situation that is creating the conditions for our stressing or angering behavior. All we can do is control our response. Then direct them to

**6.5   New Behavioral Car**

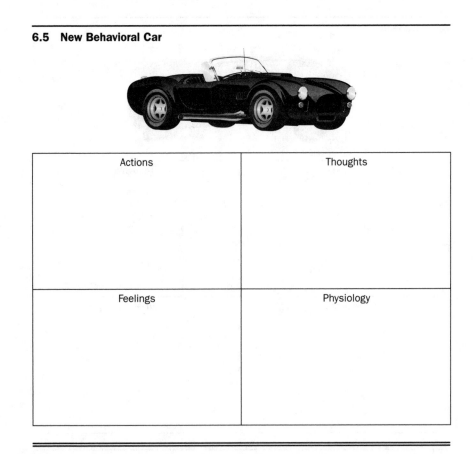

| Actions | Thoughts |
|---|---|
| | |
| Feelings | Physiology |
| | |

write down the feelings they would realistically like to experience in that same situation. They may want to write something like "calm" or "stress-free," or they may simply keep the same feeling they had in their trade-in, just to a lesser degree or intensity. Next, have them write down, in the physiology block, how their bodies would respond if they were experiencing the feelings they just listed.

7. The next two steps are the most important. You might want to briefly review with the students that it is the front wheels of their behavioral cars that they can directly control, and in so doing they can achieve the feelings and physiology they listed. First, they need to replace the thoughts they have in their trade-in with thoughts that will reduce or eliminate their stress or anger. Students will need some coaching in this step. You might coach students to replace *fear of failure thinking* or *fear of others' reaction thinking* with the following kinds of thoughts:

- Thousands of students have learned this before. I can, too.
- We all can learn, but we do so at different rates. I will get it.
- I'm good at _____, and will learn this, too.
- It wasn't easy to learn ____, but I did it.
- I have all the help and support I need to learn this.
- Other people are more worried about how they look than about me.
- In a year (a month, a week) no one will even remember this.

Students can replace *trapped thinking* with thoughts like these:

- There is always a way out.
- This, too, shall pass.
- With time and effort (and maybe a little help), I will solve this problem.

Students who engage in *catastrophizing* can be coached to examine the accuracy of their thoughts. For example, will their lives be truly ruined if they don't learn algebra as easily as their classmates? Another tack is to help them list all the personal traits, talents, support systems (including the teacher), and assets that they have that will prevent the worst from coming true. Have them list all of those resources in their thinking box: "I am a hard worker, have a supportive teacher, have good communication skills," and so on. It's remarkable how thoughts that challenge and negate the catastrophic thinking can reduce a person's stress level.

If the situations the students identify are those that arouse anger, you might coach them to challenge the truth or accuracy of their thoughts. Is it accurate to say, "I'm *always* blamed for *everything* in this classroom?" or that the teacher is "a *complete* _____"? Probably not. It's more likely that the student is *sometimes* blamed for *some* things in the classroom, and everyone has both good points and flaws. The more accurate thoughts may not totally alleviate the anger, or students may still believe that their original thoughts are accurate, so they may need to practice other thoughts that ease its intensity. Refer them to the thoughts listed above in the Tune-up section, or have them develop some on their own.

8. The next step is to help students identify the actions they could take that would result in a more positive outcome than their trade-in behavior. You might coach them by asking, "If you were thinking these new thoughts, and feeling _____ (emotions) and _____ (physiology), what responsible and effective actions might you take?" These might include breathing deeply, taking a walk, exercising, talking calmly to someone, meditating, journaling, playing music, drawing, practicing karate—anything that would redirect their stressful or angry energy in a positive direction.

9. Finally, have students review their new behavioral car and, as they did with their trade-in, give it a name. I might give them some ideas: Calm Convertible, SUV (Serene, Unruffled Vehicle), or Cool Cadillac. Have them place their two behavioral cars side by side and ask them, "Which of these cars is going to take you where you want to go, in both the short term and long term?"

Explain to students that it will be easier for a while to jump back into their old car, their old habitual behavior, when they begin to feel stressed or angry. Getting into their new car, changing their behavior when the road gets rough, takes time and practice. It usually takes between 21 and 28 days to replace an old habit with a new one. You might invite students to review their new car strategies daily for a few weeks. Or you might pair students up and have them practice their three-step Instant Tune-up process. They might even journal about how successful they are in changing to the new behavior. Sharing your own challenges and successes will help them see that achieving complete self-control is a journey that we are all on. It's also important to explain that they are going to fall back on their less effective behavior from time to time. The objective is not for them to be perfect in controlling themselves but to be better at it. As a colleague of mine, Dr. Nancy Buck, says, better is better!

## Curriculum Connections

### English and Language Arts

BACKSEAT/FRONT SEAT ESSAY: A great way to engage students in the writing process and help them see writing as meaningful is to assign students to write first-person nonfiction narratives. They know and are interested in the topic—it's all about them. You might ask the students to write about a time they allowed their back wheels (powerful emotions or physiology) to "drive" their choices. Have them analyze the outcomes of the choices they made. Then have them discuss an alternative choice they might have made if they had been in the front seat of their behavioral car and hypothesize what might have been the results.

THE ROAD NOT TAKEN: When students personally connect to characters and events in literature and history, the curriculum comes alive. After students read about a difficult decision faced by a character in a short story or novel, a figure in a history text, or a person in news article, present the students with Robert Frost's poem "The Road Not Taken" (Frost, 1975). In a class meeting, help students make connections between what they have learned about making choices (the behavioral car) and what the poem's persona has learned about choices in life. Next, discuss the difficult choice the person or people in your reading faced, the choices they made, and their consequences. Next, you might have the students complete one of the following assignments:

- Write about a difficult choice they have made that might subsequently make all the difference in their lives.

- Write about choices in their future that will have a profound impact on their lives.

- Write about the decision faced by the fictional, historical, or contemporary character in the class reading, the choice he or she made, and the results or effects of that choice. Furthermore, discuss alternate choices he or she may have made and the possible consequences of those choices.

- Provide the students with a list of fictional characters, historical figures, or people involved in current events who have faced difficult and significant decisions. Then ask your students to read the literature, historical documents, or periodical literature and complete an assignment like the one just described.

- Write a prediction of the choices a literary character might make during the reading of a novel or short story, analyzing their possible results.

PUBLISH: The final drafts of any of these narratives or essays might be published in a class magazine (perhaps called *Choices*, in either hard copy or electronic format) or extended into a speaking and listening assignment. Students would orally present their stories or papers individually or in panel discussions. Audience members might have an advanced organizer or questionnaire to complete during or after each oral presentation to help them practice focused listening skills.

### Health

Students might be assigned to do some research on the mind-body connection, studying topics such as these:

- The physical, mental, and emotional effects of stress in general
- Psychosomatic illness
- Panic attacks
- Cognitive-behavior therapy
- Stress reduction
- Antidepressants
- Benefits of meditation
- Major causes of stress

Have students gather information on the topic and develop a written and/or oral report, a PowerPoint presentation, a class DVD, a live or video skit, or a Web site dedicated to mind-body health issues.

## Conclusion

The advantages for students of understanding and applying the concept of total behavior or the behavioral car are immeasurable. Understanding the interrelationship of their thoughts, actions, feelings, and physiology will enable them to take responsibility for and self-regulate many aspects of their behavior throughout their lives. These self-regulation skills have the capacity to positively and profoundly affect students' physical and mental wellness, the quality of their relationships, their ability to learn and perform academically, and, most important, their effective functioning later in life as independent adults.

The behavioral car is an easy-to-learn metaphor that helps people increase their emotional intelligence and enhance their ability to self-regulate. In teaching these concepts to students, teachers learn them better themselves, empowering them to more effectively cope with the daily stress of teaching. (And if you are an educator, I don't have to tell you how stressful teaching can be at times.) Teachers make hundreds, maybe thousands, of decisions (choices) every day. Being able to manage their own emotions and remain calm and rational when students are being disruptive or disrespectful will make for a safer, more peaceful learning and teaching environment for everyone.

Teachers may even take themselves through the Instant Tune-up or Trade-in activities and develop effective thinking and action plans for difficult situations they anticipate in the classroom or school. When I was a first-year teacher, a volatile high school student I'll call Chris reacted to a writing assignment by telling me to do something incredibly rude and crude. I let my anger (back wheel behavior) get the best of me, and I publicly humiliated him before sending him to the principal's office. I was never able to reconnect with Chris, I lost some respect from some of my other students, and I lost quite a bit of sleep. That's not what I went into teaching for, and that certainly was not the kind of person I wanted to be. So I vowed to myself never to do that again. While that incident was still fresh in my mind, I learned about the behavioral car. I did a modified Trade-in activity in my mind and made a plan. As a high school teacher, I knew that inevitably some student would eventually say something that would push my buttons, and I wanted to be prepared.

I got a chance to drive my new behavioral car when I asked another hot-tempered boy, Darren, to stop shoving his buddy into oncoming students in the hallway. Coincidentally, he told me to do the same thing the first student did. This time, instead of losing my temper, I was able to hop into the front seat of my new car. My first thought was one I had planned for: simply "Stay cool!" Then I took a breath and thought, "Isn't it interesting how Darren is trying to make me lose it?" I smiled to myself, leaned in a little, and said calmly and quietly, "Darren, what you told me to do is totally out of the question." He gave me a sheepish smile. Then I invited him to my classroom where we had a conversation about self-control and mutual respect. In the end, he admitted he was way out of line, apologized sincerely, and learned something in the process.

Some of my colleagues thought that I should have written him up and made sure he was punished. I had talked to Darren about that option, but what was more important to me was that something change *within* Darren than that something happen *to* Darren. I told him that if I didn't see or hear any more irresponsible behavior for two weeks, I would just tear up the referral. I think Darren respected me more for the way I handled it. He was always respectful to me in the hallways after that; and later on, when I had Darren in senior English class, he was never a behavior problem. He even asked me to sign his yearbook. The important point is that using the Trade-in process turned what might have escalated into a serious discipline incident into a mutually beneficial experience: It was a personal victory for me, in that I remained calm and in control throughout. Also, I developed a positive relationship with an influential student. Darren was able to see what self-control and respect look and sound like and learned a little about his behavioral car in the process.

An additional benefit is that once teachers become familiar with these concepts and skills, they use them and teach them to people in their personal lives. They may tune up their behavioral car so that they don't get into an argument with their spouse. Or they may teach their own children the car analogy, increasing their emotional intelligence and self-efficacy. Or they may use the Trade-in process to deal with a difficult in-law or neighbor. Using these skills in their personal lives also benefits them professionally, because people who are feeling in control and balanced in their personal lives perform better at work.

Finally, as students become more skilled at self-management, you will spend less time dealing with distractions and disruptions, and more time doing what teachers really want to do: teach!

When students have learned about and practiced driving their behavioral cars, the whole class benefits. There is a common language that students begin to use with their teachers and each other. I've observed classrooms where students ask other students questions like "Are you in the back or front seat?" effectively helping each other self-evaluate and self-regulate. Classrooms in which emotional intelligence and, therefore, self-efficacy are high are calmer, more peaceful places where stress is reduced and anger is rare. The students in these classrooms have to endure far less disruption and fewer discipline incidents. The whole class then can spend more time focused on quality learning.

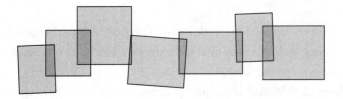

# 7 | THE PROCESS FOR POSITIVE CHANGE: CREATING THE VISION, REFLECTING, SELF-EVALUATING, AND PLANNING

*A novice Buddhist monk walked into the Zen Pizza Parlor and ordered "one with everything." Upon receiving his pizza, which came to $14.50, the young monk paid the Zen master pizza maker with a $20 bill. After waiting for an inordinate amount of time, the young monk inquired, "Excuse me, Sensei, but where is my change?" After a brief pause, the old man responded, "Change, my son, must come from within."*

The Zen master's reminder to the young monk, intended above simply as a punch line, takes on more serious implications when considered in terms of education. One definition of *learning* is "a modification or change in behavior due to experience" (*Merriam-Webster*, 1996, p. 665). No matter how skilled the instructor or how engaging the lesson plans, learning—a change in perception or behavior—must originate from within the mind and heart of the student. Unless he or she is willing or has the desire to change, no learning will take place. This is where the analogy of the Head, the Heart, and the Hand takes on additional significance. If we want students to behave (the Hand) more responsibly, for example, it takes more than knowledge (the Head) of what it means to be responsible. It takes the Heart, the desire or motivation, to behave responsibly.

This chapter introduces a process that brings the Head, Heart, and Hand together. Originally labeled *reality therapy* (Glasser, 1975), it has evolved into what Glasser (2000) now calls *counseling with choice theory*. One problem with the terms *therapy* and *counseling* is that they may lead readers to perceive of this process as one designed solely for mental health professionals. Although it is widely used to help people with a variety of psychological or emotional problems, it can also be used to help anyone interested in achieving meaningful goals and gaining effective control over his or her life. To avoid the misperception associated with the terms *therapy* and *counseling*, I will refer to this strategy as the *process for positive change* (PPC).

## The Comparing Place

The PPC involves bringing to the conscious level a procedure that human beings experience nonconsciously all of their lives. This process occurs in what Glasser (1986) calls "the comparing place." In this comparing place, a person goes through the process of comparing what she wants with what she is currently experiencing. In terms of choice theory, she is comparing a Quality World picture (her wants or goals in any given situation; see Chapter 3) with her current perception of reality (see Chapter 5). If the current perception and the Quality World picture match, she is content; and because what she is doing is achieving her goals, she will generally continue to behave as she has been. Conversely, if there is a significant mismatch between what she wants and what she is currently experiencing, she will feel a "frustration signal" (Glasser, 1986), an urge to behave in a way that will get her more of what she wants.

For example, a teacher's Quality World picture might be for all of his students to be actively engaged in a learning unit and achieve mastery on a performance assessment. If, when he teaches the unit, all of his students are actively involved and everyone achieves a *B* or better on the assessment, chances are the next time he teaches that same unit, he will follow the same lesson plans.

If, however, he finds that many students are disengaged, maybe even bored and disruptive, and after the assessment he discovers that half of his students are not successful, he will feel this frustration signal, making it likely that the next time he teaches (or reteaches) this unit, he will modify his approach.

The comparing place is analogous to a set of scales. On one side of the scales is our goal or Quality World picture. On the other side is what we are currently experiencing. When the scales are balanced, life is good. When they are out of balance, we feel frustration. Once we behave in a new way, we use our sensory system to assess whether our new behavior was effective. This noncon-scious feedback loop operates all the time, in every situation in our lives.

An important point: Just because a person feels the frustration signal doesn't mean she necessarily does something about it; or if she does choose to change, it doesn't mean that the new behavior is effective. It just means she feels the *urge* to do something. Another name for this urge or frustration signal is stress. Many people experience tipped scales in many aspects of their lives without making any changes; they just accept or put up with the degree of stress they experience: unhappy marriages, unsatisfying jobs, lack of physical fitness, and poor grades, to name a few. Even in the situations I have used as examples, teachers may simply write off the students' poor performance as the students' problem, not theirs.

As I said earlier, the PPC brings this comparing process to a conscious level, helping people intentionally look in the mirror, clearly explore their wants and goals, and evaluate their current thoughts and actions. This process helps tip their scales to the point that they will sincerely want to make a change. And once they have determined that they are willing to change, the PPC helps them make effective and attainable plans. This chapter will explain the process for positive change, discuss ways teachers can use it with students, and explain how to teach this process to students in ways that they can use it to improve their own lives and become the people they want to be.

## Objectives for Educators and Others Who Work with Students

The process for positive change can help educators and youth workers

- Manage students who are experiencing behavioral or academic problems.
- Teach students important self-evaluation skills.
- Increase student voice in the learning environment and curriculum.
- Help students articulate their vision and values.
- Achieve their own personal and professional goals.
- Plan more effectively.

- Keep meetings focused and efficient.
- Articulate their own vision and the values they choose to guide them in their personal and professional lives.

## Introducing the Process for Positive Change

The PPC incorporates all the components of choice theory (the basic human needs, the Quality World, the concept of perceptions, total behavior, and the comparing place) into a coherent, solution-based process that has been shown to be effective as a counseling, teaching, and managing strategy (Wubbolding, 2000). The PPC has two major parts. One involves the emotional environment in which the procedure is implemented. The other involves the procedure itself, a series of questions that help align one's behavior with one's goals.

### Part I: The Emotional Environment

In order for the procedures that lead to positive change to work, the emotional environment must contain trust and a sense of emotional and physical safety. A student's willingness to answer honestly and without fear the questions the teacher (or "helper") asks requires a positive, trusting relationship. This is another rationale for intentionally building and maintaining relationships as part of your ongoing teaching or managing style.

When employing the PPC with students, it's important to avoid sarcasm, overt or implied threats, criticism, and patronization. Students also need to know that what they say will be kept confidential. You may be talking about an issue that doesn't seem sensitive to you, but it may be a big deal to them. Be aware of your body language as well; sitting with the student at about the same eye level, with no big desk in the way, is optimal. You want to minimize your power differential. Also, never try the PPC when either you or the student is in an emotionally charged state. When someone is angry or highly frustrated is not the time to try to have a rational conversation. Wait until cool heads prevail.

To break the ice, just ask some nonthreatening questions. The basic human needs provide topics that anyone can relate to:

- What are some things you do for fun?

- Where is a place you like to go in your free time?
- If you didn't have to worry about money, what's something you would do every day?
- Who are some people who make you laugh?
- Where do you feel important?
- What are your favorite and least favorite subjects?
- What is something you are good at?
- What is one of your favorite foods?
- Where can I get a good pizza around here?

Once you get the sense that a positive emotional environment is set, then you can begin the procedures that lead to positive change.

## Part II: The Process

The process I'm about to describe may seem linear as I describe it, and it may work well for you if you use it in that way. You also may find that a conversation with a student takes on a life of its own, and you find yourself bouncing from one set of questions to another and back again. That's OK. The main thing to keep in mind is to address all four question sets at some point during the conversation.

A good mnemonic device to remember the kinds of questions to ask is radio station WDEP (Wubbolding, 1991). The radio station's call letters stand for questions that address

- W—what the person *wants*
- D—what the person is *doing* in relation to getting what he or she wants
- E—an *evaluation* of the effectiveness of his or her behavior
- P—a *plan* that will help him or her achieve what he or she wants

Before going on, let's take a closer look at each of these sets of questions.

### What Do You Want?

The first line of questioning concerns the subject's Quality World. The purpose of these questions is to create a vision, a mental picture in the student's mind of a target to shoot for. Without a clear target, I tell students, chances are you won't hit the bull's-eye. Your arrow (your life) may not even go in the right direction. Having a vivid picture—even better, a video—increases students' motivation to work toward it. If people don't have a clear goal in mind, their motivation is lackluster at best. But if people have a vivid vision of what they want to achieve, and all the ways that achieving that vision will add quality to their lives, then they are willing to work, persist, and endure difficulties in order to achieve that goal. On days that I find it hard to get out of bed and go for my morning run, I tell students that I think about my long-term goals: to be in shape, to look and feel healthy, to live long enough to enjoy my grandchildren and maybe even retirement. I even try to picture in my mind's eye what I want to look and feel like at 70 years old. Then I might picture the alternative. That gives me the incentive to get up, put on my running shoes, and get started.

With students, having a clear goal is equally important, whether it is what a quality presentation will look and sound like or what character traits they would like to exhibit. It's one thing for high school freshman Jasmine to simply say, "I want to be responsible." It's quite another for Jasmine to say, "Being a responsible person will help me do well in school, be successful in extracurricular activities, gain the respect of my teachers and peers, stay out of trouble at home and in school, help me get into and succeed in the college of my choice, become financially comfortable, be a good role model for others, attract a desirable mate, and maybe even make the world a better place." In the first case, the student may be just parroting what she knows adults want to hear. If that is the case, she won't be putting in a lot of effort. If, as in the second case, she sees clear short- and long-term benefits, she is much more likely to work hard and persist in efforts to become responsible.

When you begin using the PPC with students, avoid asking the generic "What do you want?" because the responses would probably be something like "candy," if you are talking to a 3rd grader; "an X-Box 360," if it's a middle schooler; or "a Hummer," if it's a high school student. Usually, your question needs to be framed for the specific situation you are focused on: "What grade do you want to shoot for in this class?" or "What kind of relationships do you want to have with your classmates?" or "What do you want (or need) that you were trying to get by disrupting class?"

It is best to begin the process with open-ended questions for two reasons. First, open-ended questions ask more of the person you are working with, giving him or her more responsibility in the process and therefore more ownership in the subsequent plan. Second, students are adept at figuring out what adults want to hear, and closed-ended questions, such as "Do you want to be successful in math class?" require little effort or thought on the part of the student. If students find it difficult to articulate what they want, you might ask what they do not want and flip their answer into something they do want. For example: "What do you *not* want in English?" The answer might be "I don't want to get kicked out of class again." Flipping that response, you might say, "So you want to stay in the classroom. Great! I want you to be there. Do you know what I need to see for that to happen?"

As I said, it's best to start out with open-ended questions, but with younger students, you might need to move to a more closed-ended approach if you don't get far with the open-ended questions: "Do you want to be thought of as a mean or kind student?" or "Do you want to keep up with your classmates in math or fall behind?" or "Do you want to complete your class work now or during choice time?"

Once you get to a general goal, it is important to not move on in the process until students have a clearer picture of how attaining this goal will increase the quality of their lives (the WIIFM approach). You might ask questions like these:

- How will your life be better for you now if you _____ (attain your goal)?
- How will your life be better in the future if you _____?
- What will be different for you if _____?
- How will things be better at home if you _____? How about at school?
- What will you have that you don't have now?
- What kind of person will you be if you _____?
- What would I see or hear if you _____?
- How will you feel if you _____?
- On a scale of 1 to 10 (10 being extremely important), how important is it for you to _____?

While the PPC works well for individuals, it can also be used with groups. With a group of students or a committee of adults, a good way to start working together is to develop a shared vision regarding both the outcome you are hoping to achieve and the behavioral norms of the group as you work toward your ultimate goals. Consider questions like these:

- What do we hope to accomplish as a group? What would it look like if we achieved our goal?
- What are the characteristics of a quality _____ (classroom, basketball team, play, band, yearbook, social studies curriculum, faculty social event, etc.)?
- What principles or values do we want to guide us as we work toward our goal?
- What attitudes and behaviors do we need from each other as we work together?
- What attitudes and behaviors do we *not* need as we work together?

Coming to consensus on a shared vision increases motivation and accountability for everyone on the team for achieving quality, and helps build relationships at the same time. Having a shared goal brings people together, and having established behavioral norms helps keep people together as they work toward their shared vision.

### What Are You Doing?

Once students have a compelling vision of their goals, the next step is to hold up a mirror to help them see what they are currently doing (or not doing) to achieve their goal as well as what they are doing (or not doing) that might be preventing them from achieving their goal. Although the focus is on their actions, this part of the process addresses total behavior, so in some cases their thoughts, feelings, and possibly physiology may be important to discuss.

For example, if I had established how being more patient with my children would add quality to my life, I might ask myself, "What am I currently doing that is helping me be more patient?" An action that is helping might be exercising daily to reduce stress in general. Another action might be taking time to play with the kids on a regular basis. Thoughts that seem to be helping me are

"Laena's 2 years old. It's developmentally normal for her to have an occasional meltdown"; "Liam is a 7-year-old boy; of course he's going to be loud and rambunctious at times." These thoughts and actions help me remain emotionally calm and physically relaxed.

What am I doing that might prevent me from being as patient as I would like? I might be trying to accomplish too many tasks in the evening or on a weekend. Maybe if I didn't have such high expectations for yard and house projects, it would be easier to take the time and be patient with my young children more consistently. Thoughts that might be getting in the way? "Why can't they just play with each other nicely so I can finish this project?" or "Why me?" or "If I hear one more whine, I'm going to lose my mind!" These thoughts tend to create irritation, frustration, and distress, which fuel physiological responses like tense muscles, raised blood pressure, and the sensation of being hot. These feelings and physiology set me up for more impatient thoughts and actions.

Jasmine, the student who wants to be more responsible, might say that some of what she is doing seems to be helping her be more responsible: keeping a calendar of assignments, club meetings, deadlines, and other important dates; doing homework before checking Twitter; and doing her chores at home without being reminded (sometimes). A thought that seems to help her is "I can do my work now and keep up with it, or get way behind, get all stressed out, and still have to do it." These actions and thoughts help her feel optimistic about her future and allow her to be physically calm, so she can sleep at night.

Some behaviors that are preventing her from achieving the level of responsibility she wants to achieve are hurrying through some homework assignments just to get them done, waiting until her mother reminds her before doing her laundry, and texting friends during class instead of listening to the teacher. Some thoughts that might be getting in her way: "This homework is stupid—nobody cares if they do a good job on it"; "Maybe Mom will forget about my laundry"; "I deserve to have a day off from track practice because I worked really hard yesterday." These thoughts sometimes create a sense of guilt and can lead to physical tension or a loss of sleep.

In working with students who are disruptive, if they are not forthcoming with the irresponsible behavior, you might simply say, "I saw (or heard) you _____." If they deny it, don't engage in arguing. That only damages the relationship and usually does not end up in their changing their story. I tell them,

"Well, that's what I saw. I don't think I hallucinate, but maybe you're right. Can we come up with a plan that will guarantee that I won't see or hallucinate that again?"

In using PPC with groups, once you've created your shared goal, you can revisit it on a regular basis and then ask, "What are we currently doing that is helping us achieve our vision? What are we doing that may be keeping us from it?" This look in the mirror is a great way to refocus discussion when it begins to wander and help people get back on track, making meetings more efficient, more productive, and less frustrating for everyone.

Traditional problem-solving processes begin with creating a vision and move right into brainstorming solutions. The PPC is based on the premise that all behavior is purposeful, so some of what we are doing and thinking must be working for us to some extent. It's important to take an honest look at our behavior so we can accurately evaluate if it is working for us to the extent that we want it to work in achieving the goal that we've articulated.

### Evaluation: How's It Working for You?

Whereas the questions so far have been open-ended (unless working with young children), the evaluation question is usually closed ended, requiring a simple yes or no. This part of the PPC is fairly short, but it often has the most profound impact on the individual we are talking to and his subsequent behavior. It simply has the individual place a value on his behavior in terms of goal achievement. Here are some useful evaluation questions:

- Is what you are currently doing helping or hurting you in achieving your goal?
- Is what you are doing going to get you what you say you want?
- How's it working for you?
- If you were to give your behavior a grade in terms of its helping you achieve your goal, would you give it an *A*, *B*, *C*, *D*, or *F*? (Follow up by asking, "What grade would you like to give it?")

Caution: Be very careful of your tone of voice and body language when you ask the evaluation question. You don't want to sound sarcastic or judgmental. Try to use as neutral a tone as possible.

Often, there is a pause before students answer these questions. That's good—they are doing some internal work. In moments like this, silence can be your friend. If the answer to the question is "Yes, it's working," the planning phase of the PPC is pretty simple. Keep doing what you have been. If the answer is "Yes, it's working for me," but the behavior they have been exhibiting is disruptive, tell them, "That behavior is unacceptable. You have a right to meet your need for freedom (or whatever need they have been trying to meet through their behavior) in this classroom, but we need to brainstorm another way for you to meet that need. Getting up and wandering around the room is too disruptive to other students."

If the answer is "No, my behavior is not getting me what I want," move on to the planning questions. You have been successful in helping students tip their scales, and they are motivated right now to change their behavior. They realize that what they are doing may be preventing them from achieving a clearly articulated goal. The Heart is now part of the equation. It's time to address the Hand. If, while you are helping them make a plan, things bog down, my rule of thumb is to go back and revisit the first set of questions: "How important is it for you to _____?" or "What is it you said you want again? How much do you want that?" This approach will often reenergize them so that they become ready to make a plan.

### What's Your Plan?

Once students have articulated a compelling goal and have looked in the mirror and evaluated their behavior, they are usually ready to make a plan. To check out their readiness, you might simply ask, "Are you ready to try something different?" If the answer is yes, have students brainstorm ideas of behaviors that are likely to be more successful. If they run out of ideas or have a limited number, ask if they would like some suggestions, adding yours on the list alongside theirs. It's important that they have choices, feel empowered in their choices, and have ownership in their plan.

Plans that have a good chance of achieving the goals students set have seven characteristics. They are simple, attainable, measurable, immediate, client centered, consistent, and committed to.

Simple: In keeping with the ancient Eastern saying, "The journey of a thousand miles begins with a single step," plans should be simple. The person doing the planning may be overwhelmed if he has to think of everything he has to do to achieve his goal. Jasmine is a good example. If she thinks of every place and time in her life she needs to be responsible, it may seem like an impossible goal. She may become so discouraged that she gives up. If, however, her plan is simple, like doing her laundry tonight without being reminded, the goal seems much more attainable. She can add to her plan later on.

Attainable: Alexandre Dumas said, "Nothing succeeds like success." If we want students to persist, their first efforts in working toward their goals should be met with success. If, for example, my plan for demonstrating greater patience with my children includes taking both of them grocery shopping with me alone late in the afternoon when we are all tired and hungry, things may not work out very well. It might be better to go shopping earlier in the day.

Measurable: A measurable plan is one that can be directly observed. It is either done or not done. It's a "do" plan, not a "don't" plan. In other words, Jasmine might say, "I won't procrastinate about homework." Not procrastinating isn't measurable. Instead, Jasmine might say, "I'll do my homework right after dinner." That is something that she can measure.

Immediate: Ideally, the first steps in an effective action plan happen immediately. The reason for that is when people evaluate that their behavior is not working in terms of achieving an important goal, it is right then that their frustration signal, their urge to act, is at its peak. Strike when the iron is hot or when the scales are out of balance. If a person waits a couple of days, the motivation to change dissipates and then he may need to go through the whole PPC over. Ask, "What are you willing to do today (or tomorrow) to get closer to your goal?"

Client Centered: The "client" is the adult, student, or group being taken through the process by the helper or teacher, the person who asks the questions. *The plan, ideally, should come from the client.* As easy and clear as it is for the helper to see what the client should do, the helper needs to do everything he or she can to *not* give his or her plan or lead the client to it. If the client does not have ownership in the plan, it is unlikely to work. Once again, developmental issues come into play. Young children in grades K–3 or 4 do not have the resources or skills to solve many of their own academic, behavior, or character issues. You might start out trying to get a plan from the student, and if she appears to be struggling, you might say, "Let's brainstorm some ideas together." And if that doesn't work, say, "Would you like some ideas from me?" Then list a few and let the student choose which one she thinks will work best. In that way the student will have some ownership in the plan.

The plan should also be *dependent on the client*. The plan should not involve other people. For example, if Jasmine's plan was to "Take care of my laundry as soon as my mother reminds me," she has an automatic excuse if the reminder slips her mother's mind. The responsibility for the client's plan must rest with the client. If you are a teacher and want to be part of the plan—for example, if the plan is to stay after school and get help with you—that's completely up to you.

CONSISTENT: The plan should be something that the client can consistently repeat. If Jasmine is more careful on her homework tonight, she can be more careful on it again tomorrow and maybe add another responsible behavior to her plan. If I succeed in remaining calm and patient taking one child to the grocery store early in the day, maybe I could try two children next week. If 3rd grader Ramone can get through the morning without blurting out an answer, he should be able to get through the afternoon. If Alicia can hand in her biology lab work on time this week, it's more likely that she will do it again next week.

COMMITTED TO: It's important to get a commitment from the client regarding his specific plan. Ask, "Are you committed to doing this?" Nail down the details: the what, when, where, and how. If the client responds with anything less than a fairly enthusiastic yes, then you might need to try to bump up the commitment. One way is to revisit the want or the Quality World picture: "How did you say your life would be better if you achieve this? Again, how important is it to you?"

Another way I've tried to bump up the commitment is to joke around a little. A common cop-out is for students to say that they will *try* to follow their plan. I'll ask, "How would you like to be on a jet flying into a foggy airport, and hear the pilot say on the intercom, 'Ladies and gentlemen, I'm going to *try* to land now!' Wouldn't you rather hear, 'We'll be on the ground in 10 minutes'?" Or, I might tell them that TRY is an acronym that stands for "Tomorrow will repeat yesterday"; in other words, if you keep doing what you've been doing, you'll keep experiencing what you've been experiencing.

## Practical Application of the PPC

The PPC is not a magic wand; it is a process that emphasizes intrinsic motivation and places responsibility for change on the client, while maintaining (sometimes improving) the important relationship between the helper and the client. If you become frustrated in helping a student develop or commit to a plan, here are some suggestions:

- Assess the emotional environment. More energy may need to go into developing a trusting relationship before attempting the PPC.

- Spend more time helping students clarify their wants and goals, their Quality World pictures. What increases motivation to change is a clear vision of their goal and the ways that achieving it will improve the quality of their lives. If you slow down and spend time focusing on their vision, the process will speed up when you get to the planning phase.

- Help students examine and evaluate the consequences of continuing their current behavior. These might be natural consequences (not learning, damaging relationships, experiencing poor health, etc.) or imposed consequences (poor grades, detention, etc.).

- Find out what they really want. Sometimes what students say they want isn't the real goal. I had a senior who did well all year and suddenly stopped working. Several conversations later, he confessed that his real goal was to avoid honoring his commitment to joining the Marine Corps upon graduation. If he didn't graduate, he couldn't be sworn in. A phone call to his recruiter solved the problem.

- If all else fails, simply impose a consequence. Some students are not willing to take responsibility and make positive changes. Meanwhile, we need to be fair and consistent.

*Note*: The first few times you attempt to use the PPC, try it with fairly compliant people. Starting with yourself is a particularly useful strategy. You will probably be fairly easy for you to work with, you get a chance to practice the questions in a safe environment, and you will add quality to your life. For example, as you drive home from work, you might pick a simple goal, like having a more relaxing evening. Think of all the ways having a more relaxing evening might benefit you, think of what you normally do, self-evaluate, and make a simple, attainable plan for making it a little bit better. Remember, perfection is not attainable, but better is better!

After you've been successful working on personal goals, try using the PPC with a fairly compliant student, then work your way up to the more resistant students. You will find that the more you use it, the more natural it will become until you find yourself integrating the PPC into your everyday thoughts and actions.

## Teaching the Process for Positive Change to Students

CHARACTER OBJECTIVES: Students will gain knowledge and skills that will help them learn responsibility, self-control, optimism, and perseverance.

SEL OBJECTIVES: Students will gain knowledge and skills that will help them with self-efficacy, self-regulation, impulse control, visioning and goal setting, self-evaluation, and effective planning.

PERFORMANCE OBJECTIVES: Students will demonstrate, through writing and role-play, the ability to use the PPC to improve the quality of their personal and academic lives.

### Teaching Strategies

As teachers know, if you really want to learn something well, teach it to others. So teaching students the PPC will help you better integrate it into your own life and simultaneously benefit students in a number of important ways.

### Class Meeting

An effective way to introduce the PPC is to have a class meeting on the topic "Success in Life." Here are some questions that might help you facilitate the discussion:

*Defining Questions*

- What does the word *success* mean?
- What does success mean to you personally?
- What does success mean to: your teachers, your friends, your parents, and your future employers?

*Personalizing Questions*

- What successes have you experienced so far: in school, in extracurricular activities, and outside school?
- How did you feel when you achieved these things?

*Challenging Questions*

- What are some of the most important successes you hope to accomplish this year? In the next few years? Later in life?

Follow this discussion by explaining that you will be teaching them a process that will make it easier and more likely for them to achieve these important successes. Explain that it is called the process for positive change, and it applies what they have learned about the basic human needs, the Quality World, perceptions, and total behavior to improving their quality of life.

### Direct Instruction

Using the explanation of the PPC earlier in this chapter to teach students the process, teach students the four major questions involved in the PPC and tie it into the SEL they have already experienced. Modify your explanation of the process to address your students' developmental abilities. Hang a poster in your room or give your students a handout of the process to put in the front of their notebooks to refer to.

### Journal Reflection

Give students a journal prompt that invites them to list some of the short- and long-term goals for themselves: getting a 100 on a spelling quiz, making the school volleyball team, getting a merit badge in Scouts, passing English, saving enough money for an iPod, achieving a black belt in tae kwon do, being promoted to first chair in the band, and so forth. Then either in the same prompt or on another day, have them pick one of their goals, analyze what they are doing to achieve it, evaluate their behavior, and make a plan.

### The Art of Listening

Pair students up with someone they will be comfortable with, but their best buddy is probably not the best partner for this activity. The Art of Listening is designed to (1) teach good active listening skills, (2) emphasize the importance of creating a clear vision when attempting to achieve a goal, and (3) help students develop good questioning skills.

STEPS

1. Designate one partner as Partner A and the other as Partner B. Have Partner A choose one of his goals, one that is important but not too emotionally charged for ethical reasons and for comfort's sake. Tell Partner B that her job is to ask questions about Partner A's goal—not how he is going to achieve it, but simply the goal itself. Tell her that she has three to five minutes to ask delving questions, and explain that it is important that she listen carefully, because when time is up, she will have to repeat back to Partner A everything that he said about his goal. You might provide students a list of questions they can choose from:

   • What do you want?

   • What would that look like?

   • What will you be doing or feeling if you attain your goal?

   • How will your life be better if you achieve your goal (at school and at home)?

   • Will attaining your goal affect any of the important people in your life? How?

- Tell me more.

- And?

- How important is it to you to achieve this goal?

- What would you have or be able to do if you achieved your goal?

- What would be some of the best things about achieving your goal?

Tell Partner B that good listeners come up with questions just by listening, being curious, and/or wanting clarification based on what Partner A says.

2. Before having the students try it on their own, model the process with a student volunteer, another adult, or, if no one is available, have some fun and play both roles yourself.

3. Set a timer for three to five minutes and let them begin. I recommend that you move around the classroom listening to the kinds of goals and questions students use, just in case some inappropriate topics or questions come up. Also, you can listen to see if students move away from simply discussing the goal to how they plan on accomplishing it. (That will come later.)

4. After the allotted time, stop them and ask Partner B to reflect back to Partner A as much about his goal as possible, including as many details as possible without adding anything to what Partner A said.

5. Have Partner A give feedback to Partner B: Was she complete? Was she accurate? Did she add anything or leave out anything? Ask Partner A how it feels to be listened to.

6. Switch roles and repeat Steps 1–4.

### Class Meeting

After the Art of Listening activity, hold a class meeting on the topic of active listening.

### Defining Questions

- What does it mean to *listen actively*?

- What other kinds of listening are there? (You might talk about *selective listening*—only hearing what you want to hear; *autobiographical listening*—listening long enough to get the gist of the message and then composing in your head a related story about you; *pretend listening*—looking at the person, nodding appropriately, saying "uh huh" at the right times, but thinking about something else entirely.)

- How do you really know someone is listening to you? (Describe attending skills like eye contact, nodding, asking probing questions, etc., but remind the class that the only sure way to know if someone is listening is if that person can paraphrase what you've said.)

### Personalizing Questions

- What was it like in the last listening activity to be listened to?
- What was it like to be the listener?
- How do you feel when people listen to you? When they don't?
- What do you think about people who listen to you? Who don't?
- Are you a good listener? Are you a better listener with some people than others?
- Do you know anyone who is a good listener?

### Challenging Questions

- Is it important to be a good listener? Why?
- Which are some places or situations when it is particularly important to be a good listener?
- Is there a place or situation in your life where it would be helpful to you to be a better listener?
- What can you do to be a better listener?

### PPC Practice

Put pairs that worked together in the Art of Listening activity to continue through the PPC. Again, model the process before asking the students to do it.

STEPS

1. The person who did the questioning first last time (Partner B) will be the "client" first this time. Partner A will (a) summarize Partner

B's want (from their last conversation) and (b) continue with the WDEP process, asking these questions:

- What are you *doing* to get what you want? What else? Anything else? Is there anything that you are doing that might keep you from getting what you want?

- If you keep doing what you're doing, will it get you what you want? (Evaluation)

- Are you willing to try something else or are you willing to keep things the way they are?

- What are some things you might do differently?

- What will you commit to doing today (or tomorrow) to achieve your goal?

2. Summarize Partner B's plan and set up a check-in.
3. Switch roles and repeat the activity.

As students are practicing, circulate among the students, coaching them and reminding the questioners to listen.

### Role-Play

Role-playing the use of the PPC helps integrate visioning, reflecting, self-evaluating, and planning skills.

THE ROUND ROBIN: A way of guiding role-play practice when students are first learning the process is to use the method known as the round robin or daisy chain. In this situation, the adult plays the client, while the rest of the class sits in a circle and plays (en masse) the helper, or questioner. One person, holding a ball, stuffed animal, or talking stick, starts the questioning process. After a question, with an optional follow-up, that person hands the talking stick to the next person or tosses the stuffed animal or ball to someone else. The next person has the option to continue the questioning in the same vein or go in a different direction, but should try to remain true to the PPC. This process continues until the teacher decides it has gone on long enough or an effective plan has emerged.

*Variation*: You might also try the split-focus approach where the adult can call time (hands in a T gesture) and switch from being the client to being a coach to the group, asking questions like "What do we know about the client's goals? What is he currently doing? How do we know these things? What parts of the PPC have we used? What questions do we need to ask next?" Then, go back into character as the client.

TRIADS: Another role-play method is to use three people in a group—the client, the helper, and a feedback observer:

- The client has a problem he or she wants to solve or a goal he or she wants to achieve.
- The helper uses the PPC to help the client.
- The feedback observer writes down the helper's questions (not the answers) and helps process the role-play when it is over. The feedback observer may also be the timekeeper.

Have students come up with a goal or a problem from a list you provide (see the examples that follow), or give them a slip of paper with the issue on it and let them role-play for anywhere from 5 to 15 minutes (3rd–4th grade, 5 minutes; 5th–8th grade, 10 minutes; 9th grade and up, 15 minutes). Tell them it is not essential to come up with a plan in that amount of time, just to stick to the process. After the allotted time, have the feedback observer say to the group, "I'm going to read the questions that the helper asked. Let's see if he or she used the process or went off track, and, if so, where and how." Next, the feedback observer reads each question, and the triad tries to identify what kind of question it was (a W, D, E, P or simply information gathering). Lastly, the feedback observer asks, "What did we learn from this role-play?" Then, if there is time, rotate roles and repeat.

Examples of role-playing problems or goals include students wanting any of the following:

- A bully to leave him alone
- To do better in math
- To stop getting in trouble for talking in class
- To get a tattoo, but her mom is against it

- To be allowed to walk to school without her dad
- To be able to borrow his dad's really nice car for prom
- To start on a varsity team
- A particular boy or girl to notice him or her
- People to stop calling him by what he thinks is a childish nickname (maybe Mattie) and call him a more mature-sounding name (Matt)
- To put together a rap group
- To go to a prestigious college
- To stop a bad habit
- To start an exercise program
- To save money for something specific
- To stop arguing with someone so much

## Curriculum Connections

### *All Subject Areas*

ACADEMIC GOAL SETTING: At the beginning of the year, ask students to answer the following questions (on a form or in a learning journal):

- Is there anything in particular you are interested in learning in this class? If so, what? Do you have any specific questions about a particular subject area?
- What kind of grade(s) do you want to achieve in this class?
- How will this class help you in your life?
- What have you done in other classes to learn what you wanted to learn?
- What have you done in other classes to receive the kind of grade you want to achieve in this class?
- Has what you've done in the past worked well for you, or do you want to try something different?
- What will you commit to doing the first few weeks of school to help you achieve and learn what you said you wanted?

If possible, conference with your students on their answers, trying to get a commitment for a mutually agreed-on academic plan. Later on in the year, if some students are struggling, you might review their plans and possibly revise them based on your conversations.

## Conclusion

The process for positive change has a variety of uses for both teachers and students. For teachers, it provides a useful process for helping students solve behavior or academic problems by taking personal responsibility and being accountable for their success. It can also help adults themselves attain important goals or overcome personal and professional challenges. It can be used by a team, a department, a faculty, or other organization to set goals, reflect, self-evaluate, and continuously improve.

Students learn a process they can use throughout their lives to increase personal responsibility for their choices; increase self-efficacy, self-regulation, and impulse control; and develop visioning, goal-setting, self-evaluating, and effective planning skills. The PPC also provides a common process for students and the adults in their lives to communicate effectively.

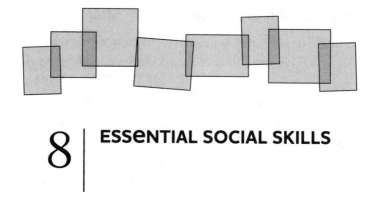

# 8 | ESSENTIAL SOCIAL SKILLS

Generally, when people are asked to reflect on the most important things in life, they list a variety of priorities: family, friends, health, work, money, their homes, their faith, hobbies, and various recreational activities. When asked the same question after a traumatic event, two items top virtually everyone's list: health and people. Interestingly, these two most important aspects of life, physical health and healthy relationships, are closely related. In Chapter 1, I introduced the three rules of education: relationships, relationships, relationships. The research I cited suggests that positive connections at school strongly influence students' attitudes about learning and encourage positive school-related behavior.

Where do we learn important social skills? As Drake Bennett (2009) of the *Boston Globe* writes, "Much of what we learn about social [and emotional] life, . . . we learn in school. The learning process is a fumbling and painful one, administered not by teachers but through schoolyard intrigues and emotional outbursts. . . . we are largely on our own" (paragraph 2). Continuing to leave the social learning process to chance is no longer acceptable. The research telling us that good social-emotional skills and strong relationships at school translate into positive attitudes about school and significantly improve academic achievement is too strong to ignore. Even if all our students' parents were intentional and consistent about teaching and modeling social skills, they still wouldn't be able to do it alone. It is time for educators to teach social skills intentionally, rather than letting it happen by chance.

## Defining Social Intelligence and Essential Social Skills

If asked to define social intelligence and social skills, most people will mention things like knowing when to say please, thank you, and excuse me; holding doors; not interrupting; chewing with your mouth closed; and so on. These are *manners*, one important aspect of social skills. Yet while a person may have been taught manners, he or she could be lacking in other important social skills. Social intelligence involves much more than just having good manners. A more general definition of social intelligence is *having the knowledge, desire, and skills to get along with others; to form and maintain positive trusting relationships; and to successfully negotiate the explicit and hidden norms, mores, and rules of society.*

This chapter will build on the foundation of emotional skills and social intelligence gained in previous chapters and provide specific strategies to teach about the following topics:

- Everyday manners
- Identification of emotions in self and others (e.g., through nonverbal cues such as facial expression, proximity, body language, tone of voice)
- Empathy
- Listening
- Assertiveness (in contrast to passivity and aggression)
- Specific social skills (e.g., interrupting appropriately, respectfully disagreeing, following instructions, accepting the nonnegotiable decisions of authorities)

You may want to teach all or just some of these skills, based on your assessment of your students' needs. Some, such as everyday manners, may be more suited to elementary students. All the others can be used as explained here or slightly modified to fit any level.

## Teaching Social Skills to Students

CHARACTER OBJECTIVES: Students will learn information and skills that will help them learn social responsibility, respect, and compassion.

SEL Objectives: Students will learn information and skills that will help them develop the ability to identify emotions in themselves and others, be assertive, self-regulate, be socially cognizant, present themselves effectively, and cooperate.

Performance Objectives: Students will demonstrate through role-playing, class meetings, and other interactive classroom strategies the ability to

- Use manners appropriately.
- Identify their own and others' emotions and attune their behavior to the latter.
- Be aware of nonverbal messages they both receive and send.
- Listen actively.
- Introduce themselves and others.
- Interrupt appropriately and disagree respectfully during conversation.
- Follow instructions.
- Accept decisions of authorities.
- Come to consensus.

## Teaching Strategies: Everyday Manners

"O tempora, O mores! Oh, the times, Oh, the manners!" exclaimed Cicero (103–42 BCE) in *Catilinam*, I:1. Over 2,000 years later, I hear similar cries in classrooms almost everywhere I go: "Students just don't seem to have any manners anymore." Then I go to restaurants and see men dining with their baseball caps on, people ordering food by saying something like, "Gimme the seafood combo" as their cell phone starts ringing, and responding to "Thank you. Come back soon!" with a grunt as they let the door close on the party exiting behind them.

It's no mystery why students are not models of etiquette. Yes, students should be learning manners at home, but they are either not learning them at home or just not practicing them at school. As educators, we can accept things as they are or teach students the basic manners they will need to use both in school and after they graduate. A good way to begin teaching these basics is through a class meeting.

### Class Meeting: Manners (and Introduction to Social Skills)

As you normally would, start the class meeting by having students sit in a circle with no furniture in the way and reviewing the ground rules for class meetings. Here are the define, personalize, and challenge questions:

*Defining Questions*

- If we were to look up the word *manners* in the dictionary, what do you think it would say?
- What are some examples of manners?
- What situations call for manners?

*Personalizing Questions*

- Are there any specific manners that you think are particularly important?
- Do you know someone who has bad manners? Please don't discuss anyone present and no names, please, but give us an example of this person's poor manners.
- How do you feel or what do you think about this person when he or she demonstrates poor manners?
- Do you know someone who has particularly good manners?
- Turn to a neighbor or two, and rate your own manners on a scale of 1–10. A 1 means no manners, that you are a social disaster area, and a 10 means that you have unusually good manners, maybe like the person or people brought up in the meeting. This means you always remember to say please, thank you, and excuse me; to open and hold doors; greet people; introduce others; and exhibit other polite behaviors.
- Where did you learn manners? Who is a particularly important influence on your manners?

*Challenging Questions*

- Do you think manners are important? Why or why not?
- What manners are particularly important in school? Why?
- What do you think school would be like if everyone (administrators; teachers; staff members like bus drivers, custodians, and cafeteria

workers; and students) could honestly rate him- or herself at least an 8 out of 10? How would it be different from what it is now?

- Would it be worth it to you to improve your manners if we could have a school like that?

Next, introduce the topic of social skills, telling students that using good manners is one kind of social skill. There are others as well: identifying emotions, yours and others'; listening effectively; having empathy, which means being able to take others' perspectives and identifying with their feelings; and behaving in specific ways in social situations, such as greeting people and introducing yourself. Tell students, "Over the next _____, we will be discussing and practicing these and other social skills."

### Direct Instruction

This section is designed for younger students and for students who have little or no familiarity with culturally accepted manners. For middle school students, the class meeting and some manners posters hung and referred to when appropriate would probably suffice. For high school students, the class meeting alone would be enough. Of course, teachers' and other adults' consistent modeling of good manners is essential to any of the lessons' success.

Begin by reviewing the important points students made about manners in the class meeting. Explain that manners are like the glue that holds society together. Explain that in future lessons, they will be learning other social skills, but today they are going to learn or review five specific manners: *Please, Thank you, You're welcome, Excuse me*, and *I'm sorry*. Show the class posters or a PowerPoint presentation that explains the situations in which you use these words or phrases. Even better, prepare a few students to model the use of the phrases as you explain them.

#### Please
Use the word *please* when you ask for something or make a request:

- May I please borrow your car?
- I would like a BlackBerry, please.
- Please pass me my guitar case.

Use it when responding positively to an offer:

- Would you like some enchiladas? *Yes, please.*
- Are you interested in interviewing for a job? *Yes, please.*

### THANK YOU

The phrase *thank you* expresses gratitude. Use it when someone gives you something:

- Thank you for letting me borrow your car.
- I love the BlackBerry. Thank you very much.

Use it when someone pays you a compliment:

- You have a great singing voice. *Thank you!*
- Your mother is a really great cook. *Thank you. I'll tell her you said so.*

Use it when someone does something for you:

- Thanks for passing me my guitar case.
- Thank you for holding the door.

Use it when turning down an offer:

- Would you like some more pizza? *No, thank you.*
- Would you like to go to the mall with us? *No, thanks, I think I'll stay home and watch a movie.*

### YOU'RE WELCOME

Use the phrase *you're welcome* when someone thanks you for something:

- Thanks for taking out the trash. *You're welcome.*
- Thank you for telling me about that cool Web site. *You're welcome.*

### EXCUSE ME

Use *excuse me*, a most versatile phrase, when you do or say something that might annoy someone—for example, when

- You walk in front of someone.
- You bump into (or almost bump into) someone.
- You interrupt someone (say, "Excuse me," then stop talking).
- You need to interrupt someone for something urgent ("Excuse me, Amber, you have a phone call").

- You walk between two people who are talking (walk around them if possible).
- You do or say something inappropriate.

## I'M SORRY

*I'm sorry*, like *excuse me*, is used when you do or say something that might bother or hurt someone else. Generally, *I'm sorry* is used for more serious mistakes than *excuse me*. Of course, it is preferable not to put yourself in a position to have to apologize, but you might use *I'm sorry* or *I apologize* when

- You hurt someone or hurt someone's feelings ("I apologize for calling you that name").
- You inconvenience someone ("I'm sorry I made you wait so long").
- You disappoint someone ("I'm sorry I forgot to return that CD to you").

*Note*: A sincere tone of voice is critical to any of these words or phrases. (See the discussion on nonverbal communication later.)

### Role-Playing Everyday Manners

STEPS

1. Arrange your students in the Inside-Outside Circle structure, giving them each an index card with a situation that calls for everyday manners. Explain that the inside circle students will read their cards to their partners in the outside circle, and the partners are to respond with the correct word or phrase in the context of the situation.

2. Next, the outside circle students will read their cards to their partners, who in turn will respond to their partners with the appropriate word or phrase.

3. After each partner has read his or her card and responded to the partner, direct partners to switch cards. Then ask one of the circles to move a certain number of places to the right (usually two or three places is effective), and repeat the process until each student has had a chance to read and respond to several different situations.

4. As the students practice, move around the circle to listen in and guide their practice, if necessary.

Here are some suggested situations for the index cards:

- What would you say if you want me to lend you a pencil?
- What would you say if you want me to stop singing so you can concentrate on your reading?
- What would you say if you would like me to help you carry your drums to the band room?
- Would you like to come with us to the Jonas Brothers concert?
- Would you like some homemade blueberry pie?
- I love your new shoes.
- You are a really good dancer.
- I just put in the DVD you asked me to.
- You were amazing in yesterday's game.
- Your hair looks really good today.
- Thank you so much for helping me with my math.
- You were really a good friend yesterday when I needed it. Thank you.
- Thanks for listening to me. I really needed that.
- Thanks for waiting for me.
- What would you say if you just bumped into someone?
- What would you say if your cell phone rang when you were in the middle of a serious conversation?
- What would you say if you needed to interrupt a teacher because there was someone at the door of the classroom that he or she didn't see?
- What would you say if you accidentally walked into the wrong classroom?
- What would you say if you were talking really loud in a crowded room, it suddenly got quiet, but you kept going for a few words?
- What would you say if you had to walk in front of someone who was looking for a video at the video store?
- What would you say if you accidentally burped out loud in public?
- What would you say if you got angry and called a friend a jerk?
- What would you say if you accidentally stepped on someone's toe?

### Teaching Strategies: Identifying Emotions in Ourselves

Being able to identify others' emotions is a skill that is absolutely essential to developing and maintaining positive relationships. It is the tap root of empathy, which is essential to the development of social intelligence. This skill is discussed in a later section, but before we can accurately identify others' emotions, we first need to identify our own. Accurately identifying our emotions can help us choose effective thoughts and actions (see Chapter 6) in a variety of situations. Misidentification of our own emotions can result in problems.

Consider the story of T.J., a normally well-behaved 4th grade student who was getting into frequent arguments and fights on the playground during recess. He'd been in lunch detention, had been in three after-school detentions, and was recently suspended for three days for starting a fistfight.

After three sessions with the school counselor, Mrs. Jackson, who was trying to discover the root of T.J.'s sudden violent streak, he blurted out that his dad was recently incarcerated and that he was "just mad" at everyone. His arguing and fighting were his way of expressing what he had identified as anger. In a subsequent counseling session, Mrs. Jackson helped T.J. realize that, yes, he was angry: at the system for putting his dad in prison and at his dad for dealing drugs, resulting in his being sent there. But underlying that anger were deeper emotions—betrayal, loss, and loneliness. (T.J. had been living with his dad and his dad's girlfriend, but now he was living with his maternal grandmother, whom he hardly knew.) Those are pretty complicated emotions for a 9- or 10-year-old boy. He couldn't accurately identify what he felt; he just knew it was bad. It was less complicated to assign that pain a label he could understand and act on—anger—than to analyze his feelings and try to find other ways of soothing himself. T.J. was referred to weekly counseling sessions, and the violent outbursts gradually disappeared.

#### Class Meeting: Identifying Our Emotions

*Defining Questions*

- How would you define the word *emotion*?
- Can you list some emotions? (Brainstorm a list on the board. If someone mentions *mad, sad, glad,* or *afraid*, write them in a specific place on the board. For 3rd and 4th graders, keep the list fairly basic, focusing on

the primary emotions: love, joy, surprise, anger, sadness, and fear. With older students, list and define, if necessary, a few more complex emotions. See Figure 8.1.)

*Personalizing Questions*

Do a WHIP here (see p. 56):

- Fill in the blank: One of my favorite emotions is _____.
- An emotion I really don't like to feel is _____.
- Do you know someone who is extremely emotional? (No one in this class and no names.) How do you know he or she is emotional?

*Challenging Questions*

- What do you think emotions are for?
- Should we let our emotions control our behavior?
- Can our emotions work against us?
- How can we use our emotions in ways that will help us? (Ideally someone will say that we should use them as signals that things are going well or not; emotions should help us choose to do something responsible that will result in improving a situation or in our feeling better. For example, if I am feeling angry, taking a walk or talking to a good friend would help me feel better. Or, if I am frustrated in doing something, I could ask someone for help.)

### Emotional Graffiti

This activity is designed for middle and high school students. Elementary students can use the next activity, Emotions and Me Graffiti, instead.

STEPS

1. Attach chart paper to the walls around the room, as equally distributed as possible, with enough room between posters to accommodate small groups of students gathered around each. Write a primary emotion at the top of each piece of chart paper: anger, sadness, joy, fear, surprise, and love (or attachment).

## 8.1 Emotions

| Primary Emotion | Love | Joy | Surprise | Anger | Sadness | Fear |
|---|---|---|---|---|---|---|
| **Secondary Emotions** | Affection<br>Longing | Cheerfulness<br>Contentment<br>Pride<br>Optimism<br>Enthrallment<br>Relief | Surprise | Irritation<br>Exasperation<br>Rage<br>Disgust<br>Envy | Suffering<br>Disappointment<br>Shame<br>Neglect<br>Sympathy | Horror<br>Nervousness |
| **Tertiary Emotions** | Adoration<br>Affection<br>Fondness<br>Liking<br>Attraction<br>Caring<br>Tenderness<br>Compassion<br>Sentimentality<br>Desire<br>Passion<br>Infatuation | Amusement<br>Bliss<br>Glee<br>Jolliness<br>Joviality<br>Delight<br>Enjoyment<br>Gladness<br>Happiness<br>Jubilation<br>Elation<br>Satisfaction<br>Euphoria<br>Enthusiasm<br>Excitement<br>Exhilaration<br>Contentment<br>Pleasure<br>Eagerness<br>Hope<br>Rapture | Amazement<br>Astonishment | Aggravation<br>Agitation<br>Annoyance<br>Grouchiness<br>Frustration<br>Fury<br>Hostility<br>Bitterness<br>Hate<br>Loathing<br>Scorn<br>Spite<br>Vengefulness<br>Dislike<br>Resentment<br>Revulsion<br>Contempt<br>Jealousy | Agony<br>Hurt<br>Anguish<br>Depression<br>Despair<br>Hopelessness<br>Gloom<br>Unhappiness<br>Grief<br>Sorrow<br>Misery<br>Melancholy<br>Dismay<br>Displeasure<br>Guilt<br>Regret<br>Remorse<br>Alienation<br>Isolation<br>Loneliness<br>Rejection<br>Homesickness<br>Defeat<br>Embarrassment<br>Humiliation<br>Pity | Alarm<br>Shock<br>Fright<br>Terror<br>Panic<br>Hysteria<br>Mortification<br>Anxiety<br>Tenseness<br>Uneasiness<br>Apprehension<br>Worry<br>Distress<br>Dread |

2. Put students in cooperative groups of three to five, give each group a marker or two, and assign each group to stand by a poster.

3. Explain to them that when you say "Begin," they are to brainstorm as many related emotions as they can. (Give a couple of examples: joy—happiness, contentment, excitement; sadness—grief, depression, etc.)

4. After two to three minutes at one poster, have the groups rotate clockwise to the next poster.

5. Repeat until every group has been to every poster.

6. Have students bring the posters to the front of the room and process what they have listed. In some cases, you may need to help them correct their examples.

7. End by displaying a poster of Figure 8.1, discussing any important emotions that students omitted from their list. You may want to leave this poster on the wall to refer to throughout the year.

### Emotions and Me Graffiti

STEPS

1. Attach chart paper to the walls around the room, as equally distributed as possible, with enough room between posters to accommodate small groups of students gathered around each. Write an emotion at the top of each piece of chart paper. For younger students, use only the primary emotions: anger, sadness, joy, fear, surprise, and love (or attachment). For older students include a few secondary emotions.

2. Put students in cooperative groups of three to five, give each group a marker or two, and assign each group to a poster.

3. Explain to them that when you say "Begin," they are to brainstorm situations (school-appropriate situations) in their lives when they have experienced these (or related) emotions.

4. After two to three minutes at one poster, have the groups rotate clockwise to the next poster.

5. Repeat until every group has been to every poster.

6. Have students bring the posters to the front of the room and process what they have listed. In some cases, you may need to help them correct their examples.

*Note:* This would be a great time to review the concept of the behavioral car (see Chapter 6).

### Emotional Continuum

Another way to help students integrate their understanding of emotions is to have them rank or grade emotions based on a certain criterion—for example, from strongest to weakest. After getting students in groups of three or four, give them a continuum sheet showing marks on the left for the weakest emotions and on the right for the strongest (see Figure 8.2). Their assignment is to fill in the continuum with emotions (based on the same primary emotion) from weakest on the left end to strongest on the right. You might give students with higher abilities one emotion to start with, tell them they can place it anywhere on the continuum they want, and remind them to refer to their graffiti poster or the poster based on Figure 8.1 to fill in the others. Or you might give lower-ability students all four emotions and ask them to arrange the emotions on the continuum. In either case, it is important that students discuss among themselves why they chose to put the emotions in the order they did. Have them present their final product to the class along with their rationale.

*Variations:* Give students a continuum with more spaces on it to place more emotions. Or choose other criteria for the continuum: least pleasant to most; least destructive to most; easiest to self-regulate when experiencing to most difficult; most frequently experienced in school to least.

---

**8.2 Emotional Continuum Example**

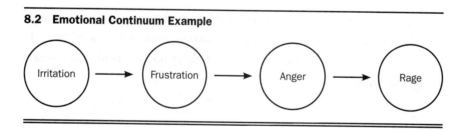

## Teaching Strategies: Identifying Others' Emotions

Just as identifying and managing our own emotions are essential to our personal well-being and happiness, being able to accurately identify others' emotions is essential to our social well-being and happiness. Being able to pick up on others' emotions can help us attune ourselves to them and more effectively communicate, manage, or work with them, and get along better with people in general. An inability to identify how people are feeling can easily lead to conflict and problems.

When I was teaching middle school, I noticed this skill deficit in a number of my students, mostly boys. During my first or second year supervising the middle school cafeteria during lunch (which I did for 11 years), students for whom I wrote referrals were those who didn't accurately read my emotions. I remember approaching one group of four boys who were playing hacky sack in one of the stairwells, which was against the rules. When I asked them to stop, three stopped, but one boy continued playing by himself and laughing, saying, "C'mon, Mr. Erwin, wanna try it?"

I gave him my best "teacher" look and said, "Seriously, Terrance, stop. It's not safe to play that here. I'm not kidding!"

But I think he thought I was. He kept on playing, laughing all the while. "It won't hurt you, Mr. Erwin. Really! Try it."

I was so angry I grabbed the hacky sack and escorted him to the office. Only when I put my hand on his elbow did he realize I was serious. "Geez, Mr. Erwin. Don't blow a gasket! I'll stop."

"Why didn't you stop five minutes ago?" I asked.

"I didn't think you meant it," he replied.

I don't think Terrance was fibbing. Since that time, I've seen the same inability to accurately identify others' emotions dozens of times, often with a similar result.

Goleman (1995) writes, "Schoolyard bullies . . . often strike out in anger because they misinterpret neutral messages and expressions as hostile" (p. 271). This section of the chapter helps us teach students how to avoid such mistakes and their consequences.

### Class Meeting: Identifying Emotions in Others

Begin the meeting by saying, "Today we're going to discuss the importance of being able to identify emotions in others. I don't think we have any terms that need to be defined, but we might need to consider whose feelings it would be important to identify and where it is important to identify emotions." Then answer the define, personalize, and challenge questions.

*Defining Questions*

- Whose emotions would it be important to identify and why?

- Why would it be important to identify people's feelings at home? At school? At work?

- Where else might it be useful to identify emotions?

*Personalizing Questions*

- Let's take the primary emotions: love, anger, surprise, fear, sadness, and joy. How would someone know when you are feeling those feelings? What does your face look like? What does your body (posture, gestures, etc.) look like? (Take each one and have students discuss, show, and model each expression. If you have a drama department at your school, see if you can get some students to come to class or create a video demonstrating facial expressions of various emotions.)

- Can we always read someone's emotions from his or her face or body language?

- Are there times you put on a "social mask," so to speak, and try to hide your feelings? Why?

- When you are feeling _____, what kind of behavior do you want or need from others?

*Challenging Questions*

- How can we use what we've discussed today about identifying others' emotions?

- How might what we discussed today benefit you?

### Direct Instruction: Facial Expressions

You might want to show your students some examples of the primary facial expressions. One can be found on a Web site called DataFace at http://face-and-emotion.com/dataface/general/homepage.jsp. Click on the Emotions tab, go to the bottom of the page, and click on Emotion Expressions. If you click on any of the faces expressing primary emotions, you will learn the general characteristics of each expression. Following are some activities for practicing facial expressions.

THE FEELING GAME: For younger students or students who have a greater need for identifying emotions from facial expressions, several Web sites are dedicated to helping them. One is www.do2learn.com, where children can practice identifying facial expressions and receive immediate feedback online.

FEELING FLASH CARDS: Go to www.mes-english.com/flashcards, where you can download feeling flash cards to help your elementary students practice. You might use the Inside-Outside Circle structure, with students swapping cards after each drill.

FEELINGS MATCH GAME: This game can be used with any age group. Invite your students to bring in magazines from home—the more variety, the better. Cut out or have students cut out pictures of people (trying to avoid including the setting the picture was taken in) expressing a variety of emotions; then mat the pictures and laminate them, if possible. Create a simple playing area by printing the six primary emotions on card stock and spreading them out on a tabletop for a small group, or on the floor in the center of a class meeting. Individually or in small groups, students discuss each facial expression and place it near the primary emotion they think it best fits. Older students might be encouraged to identify the secondary or tertiary emotion expressed. Then the students might discuss their choice. What is it about the facial expression that suggests that emotion? Is there any body language involved?

### Direct Instruction: Body Language

Explain that only a small percentage of the messages we send when we interact with others is through spoken words. As we've already seen, our facial expressions say a lot. So do our bodies—through posture and gestures. Demonstrate yourself, or have students or another adult you've rehearsed with demonstrate, how posture and gestures communicate messages nonverbally by showing the following emotions:

| | |
|---|---|
| Sadness | Fear |
| Excitement | Contentment |
| Anger | Confidence |
| Impatience | Exhaustion |
| Illness | Confusion |

### Acting 101

As a large group, have students demonstrate, using only their facial expression and gestures, the feelings or moods you call out. Call out each of the following (or others), and give them some time to act out the emotion or mood:

| | |
|---|---|
| Happy | Worried |
| Sad | Frustrated |
| Scared | Puzzled |
| Angry | Thrilled |
| Impatient | Exhausted |
| Proud | Surprised |

*Variation 1*: Give individual students cards with emotions listed on them. Have them act out the emotion for 10 seconds. Tell students not to blurt out the emotion, that they will have a chance to identify what they see. After the time is up or the actor is through, ask students, "What is the emotion _____ is expressing?" and "What gave it away?"

*Variation 2*: For younger students, give each student a set of index cards with the primary emotions, one emotion per card. Act out an emotion for up to 10 seconds, then say, "What's my emotion?" and have the students hold up the card with the emotion they think you are expressing. Again, ask them what you did that gave it away.

### Class Meeting: Proximity

Another aspect of nonverbal communication is proximity, the distance one person is from another during a conversation. You might hold a class meeting about proximity, in which you do some direct instruction as you go.

*Defining Questions*

- Explain that proximity is the distance between people in different situations.

- Do different situations call for different proximity? For example? (Students' answers might include statements such as: friends are more comfortable being closer than acquaintances; people at a crowded concert or movie theater are more comfortable being close than people in a restaurant; girls are more comfortable being close than boys, except in contact sports; informal social conversation is more comfortable at a greater distance than an intimate conversation between good friends or a couple.

*Personalizing Questions*

- Have you ever been in a conversation where you felt uncomfortable because the person you were talking to was too close? Too far away?

- How might proximity affect the way you perceive someone's emotions or intentions?

*Challenging Question*

- What do you think a good rule of thumb is for conversational proximity? (In the United States and northern Europe, about an arm's length is generally considered comfortable for friendly acquaintances. You might mention that in other cultures, closer or more distant proximity may be the norm. If you have students from other cultures, ask them to share their perceptions of proximity across cultures.)

### Direct Instruction: Tone of Voice

Explain how important tone of voice is to communication. Demonstrate this by using the same phrase and achieving several different meanings out of it by changing your tone of voice. You might use the sentence "I really love riding my brother's bike to school in the rain." Say it these different ways:

- Sincerely
- Sarcastically
  - With the accent on "love"

- With the accent on "school"
- With the accent on "in the rain"

• Enthusiastically
   - With the accent on "really love"
   - With the accent on "my brother's"
   - With the accent on "in the rain"

• As a question

• With no energy at all

• Any other way you can change the meaning

Discuss all the variations of meaning that can come from the same 12 words. You might have students try it with a partner, using the sentence "I really like watching news on TV." Ask a few talented actors to demonstrate the different meanings they can achieve through tone of voice alone.

### Peas and Carrots

Develop a set of index cards with a variety of emotions and attitudes on them: angry, sarcastic, silly, thrilled, conceited, frustrated, serious, unsure, happy, scared, and so on. Pair students up and pass out an index card to each student. Direct students to practice using the appropriate voice tone for the situation on their card, using only the phrase "Peas and carrots" repeated as necessary (you might want to model). Have some students demonstrate for the whole class.

### Direct Instruction: Attuning to Others' Emotions

Review with students how facial expression, body language, gestures, and tone of voice can provide important clues as to someone's emotional state. Also review why it is important to determine someone's emotional state when interacting with him or her. Next, teach the steps one can use to attune oneself to another person's emotional state:

1. Notice the situation that is occurring.

2. Observe the other person's facial expression, voice tone, and gestures.

3. Think about what feelings you are experiencing when you demonstrate similar behaviors.

4. Assess the other person's current mood or emotions.

5. If appropriate, check out your assessment with him or her ("Are you feeling frustrated right now?").

6. Ask yourself, "What behaviors do I need from people around me when I'm feeling _____?"

7. Attune your behavior to the person's emotional state.

## Teaching Strategies: Empathy

*Empathy* is "the action of understanding, being aware of, being sensitive to, and vicariously experiencing the feelings, thoughts, and experiences of another" without actually experiencing what the other person did (*Merriam-Webster*, 1996, p. 378). In a minilecture, you might want to take apart the definition of empathy and help students understand what empathy is and is not. Then you might go on to explain that empathy is a catalyst for effectively interacting, communicating, and getting along with people at school or work, at home, and at play.

Empathy provides the impetus for using manners and other social skills well. Without empathy, social skills feel and seem artificial. As most adults know, developing empathy takes time and intentionality. While identifying emotions in ourselves and others provides a necessary foundation for promoting empathy, guided and independent practice is essential to its full maturation. Regularly taking others' perspectives in a variety of situations is particularly helpful in developing this important skill.

### Narrative Perspective Taking

The "Curriculum Connections" section of Chapter 5 explains several ways of helping students examine varying perspectives of literary, historical, or current events. You can also give students hypothetical situations and ask them to identify and empathize with the thoughts, feelings, and perspectives of different people in the situation. Here are some examples:

*A single working mother, Charon, is trying to put her 4-year-old Chloe to bed on a weekday night. She got up at her normal time, 6:00 a.m., dropped Chloe off at the babysitter, worked all day, and then attended a meeting with her boss after work, where she was told that because of the company's financial troubles she would have to take on more responsibilities but receive the same pay. She didn't get home until 6:00 p.m. She then made dinner for herself, Chloe, and her 10-year-old son Miles. Miles told his mom at dinner that he needs help with his math homework. Charon and her children live in an apartment building next door to Mike, a struggling artist who has to work two jobs to make ends meet. One of his jobs is delivering newspapers, which requires him to get up at 4:30 a.m. so he can get his papers delivered before he goes to his second job. It is now 8:00 p.m., and Chloe is throwing a loud tantrum.*

Try to empathize with each of the following people, identifying what they might be thinking and how they might be feeling based on the situation described here. What might they be saying or doing?

- Charon
- Charon's boss
- Miles
- Chloe
- Mike

*It's January 23. Eighth grader Lashara is about to go to her first day in a new middle school in an upscale suburb of Boston. She and her family just moved there from Atlanta, where they lived in an apartment in the city. Lashara is quiet and shy. When she woke up this morning, she looked in the mirror and noticed a big pimple on her forehead. Kendra, Lashara's overprotective mother, in an attempt to ease Lashara's transition to the new school, has arranged for Rachel, a neighbor's daughter whom Lashara has only met once briefly, to walk to school with Lashara. Brad, Lashara's dad, disagreed with Kendra about this arrangement, but Kendra insisted. Besides, Brad was running behind this morning, his first day at his new job. He didn't have time to argue with her. Rachel is one of the most popular girls in her class and has a morning ritual of hanging out at her locker with several other popular girls. She was informed of the arrangement five minutes before she left for school.*

What might the following people be thinking and feeling this morning? What kinds of things might they say or do?

- Kendra

- Lashara

- Brad

- Rachel

- Rachel's mother

You might develop scenarios of your own or have students, in small groups, develop their own vignettes and give them to another group to analyze and empathize from different perspectives.

### Photo Perspective Taking

Another approach to perspective taking is to show to students a photograph of people in various situations and ask them to try to take the perspective

---

**8.3  What Is She Thinking?**

of different people in the photograph. For example, for the photo in Figure 8.3, you might ask students to write down what they think the girl is thinking and feeling and why. There are several royalty-free photograph and image sites online from which to download photographs.

## Teaching Strategies: Empathetic Listening

Empathetic listening continues where the listening exercise in Chapter 7 left off. In fact, you might want to revisit the class meeting from Chapter 7 before introducing the topic of empathetic listening.

### Direct Instruction: Empathetic Listening

Define *empathetic listening* as active, deep listening, the sole intention of which is to understand the thoughts, feelings, and experiences of another person in a way that allows us to vicariously experience them. (You might need to remind them of other kinds of listening—selective, autobiographical, etc.)

### Musical Circles

I learned Musical Circles from a colleague, Diane Vance, director of Smart Character Choices in Howell, Michigan.

STEPS

1. Write the questions on pp. 174–175 or others you devise on index cards.

2. Give each student an index card and tell the students that they are going to engage in empathetic listening practice. Define empathetic listening for them and explain that this skill, combined with perspective taking and emotion identification, will take them a long way toward the social skill of empathy.

3. Explain that you will be playing some lively dance music. While the music is playing, they are to move and mix around the room. Dancing is optional. When the music stops, they are to freeze, then find the partner closest to them. Remind them that their goal will be to talk to different people in each pairing, so they shouldn't just follow their friends around.

4. Play the music for 20–30 seconds, then stop and say, "Freeze!" Direct students who do not have a partner to raise their hands.

5. Ask the students to determine who is Partner A and who is Partner B.

6. Say, "Partner A, read your question to your partner." Partner B has 30 seconds to respond. After 30 seconds, Partner A will try to summarize what Partner B said and identify the emotion he expressed. (With younger students, focus on primary emotions; with older students, challenge them to identify more subtle emotions—secondary and tertiary.)

7. Have Partner A and B switch roles, so that this time A is listening and summarizing what B says in response to A's question.

8. Have students trade their cards, play the music, and repeat three or four times.

You might use some of the following prompts during the activity:

1. Describe a time you could not stop laughing.

2. Tell about a time you were sad.

3. What is something you are proud of—something you do well, you've accomplished, or you own?

4. Tell about a time you were scared.

5. Describe something that makes you mad.

6. What is something that bothers you about this school?

7. What is one of your favorite memories of school?

8. Who is a teacher you've really liked and why?

9. Tell about a time a friend or family member made you laugh.

10. Where is a place you don't like to go? Tell about it.

11. Have you ever had a big surprise? Tell about it.

12. What is one of the happiest times of your life? Tell about it.

13. At home, what is something that frustrates you?

14. Has a family member ever done something that made you mad? Tell about it.

15. Is there anything that scares you? Why or why not? Talk about it.

16. When was the last time you were really sad? Why?

17. When was the last time you were really excited? Why?

18. When you were little, what is something that you got really excited about?

19. When you were little, who or what made you laugh really hard?

20. When you were little, what scared you?

21. What is something you look forward to in your future? Why?

22. Is there anything that worries you about the future? What and why?

23. What are the characteristics you look for in a friend?

24. What are the characteristics you will look for in a future mate?

25. Has anyone ever been envious of you, or have you ever envied anyone else? Tell about it.

Some of these questions might bring up strong emotions in students, so this activity requires a trusting environment in the classroom. Unless there is a supportive atmosphere, the questions may fall flat or even create behavioral or emotional problems. If, however, you have been using the ideas and strategies in this book (or other relationship-building activities), your class should enjoy and learn from this activity.

Ask students what they learned about empathetic listening during the activity. Did they like it when they were doing the talking? Why or why not? Did they enjoy doing the listening? Why or why not? What was the best thing about it? What was the hardest? When might they need to use empathetic listening in their lives again?

*Variation*: You could also use the Inside-Outside Circle structure (see Chapter 2) for this activity (no music necessary).

### Class Meeting: Empathy

This class meeting is suited best to grades 5 and up. Start by addressing these questions:

*Defining Questions*

• In your own words, what is *empathy*?

- You might need to help clarify with more closed-ended questions: Do you have to have experienced the same thing as the other person to empathize? (Explain that no, you only have to *understand* how that person might have thought, felt, and behaved and to *vicariously* experience what he or she did.)
- What skills help you become empathetic? (Examples include identifying emotions in self and others, listening.)

### Personalizing Questions

- Do you know someone who is empathetic? What gives you that impression?
- What do you think of this person?
- Have you ever known someone who seems to lack empathy? (No one in this room and no names.) What gives you that impression?
- What did you think or feel about this person?
- Turn to a partner and tell him or her how empathetic you think you are on a scale of 1 to 10 (1 being Hitler, 10 being Gandhi). What number would you like to give yourself? Why? What do you need to do to get there?

### Challenging Questions

- Can you disagree with someone and still be empathetic toward that person? Give examples. (Try to encourage students' personal responses. You might provide an example of your own. For example, I might tell students that when I was in the army, I *disagreed* with my drill sergeant's way of speaking to me and my platoon buddies, but I could *empathize* with him. It must have been incredibly frustrating to be charged with molding the sad lot of about 50 mostly 18-year-old boys, who'd never been away from Tuscaloosa or Spokane or Detroit or Jersey City or whatever small town they enlisted in, into a disciplined unit of men—and have only seven weeks and three days to do it. So I understand how he might think he needs to bellow unprintable names at us day and night.)
- Is it possible to empathize with someone you not only disagree with but really dislike? Examples? (No one in the class and no names.)

- In what ways might it help our community (city, country, world) if there were more empathy? What is preventing people from being more empathetic? What can we do about it?

## Teaching Strategies: Assertiveness

Much of this chapter has been devoted to empathy and attuning ourselves to others' emotions. Those attitudes and skills are very important, but there are times when we need and want others to attune themselves to *our* needs and wants: if they are in our personal space, for example, or if they are in some way treating us disrespectfully or irresponsibly, or if we simply need something from them. We may use three general approaches at such times; the first two are as follows:

- Being *passive*, which is really doing nothing or very little. It is accepting or enduring the status quo, hoping that something outside us will change—the person bothering us will go away, for example, or move on to bother someone else if she doesn't get a reaction from us.

- Being *aggressive*, which is being combative, severe, or hostile in pursuing one's self-interest—for example, speaking overly harshly to or being violent with someone who may be bothering us. "The best defense is a strong offense" is the aggressor's philosophy.

There are problems associated with each of these approaches. Passive people may come to see themselves as helpless pawns, controlled by other people and their environment, which may in turn lead others to treat them that way, creating an endless cycle of victimization. Aggressive people are often socially and emotionally ostracized and isolated. If aggressive children become aggressive and violent adults, there is a good chance they will be incarcerated. The middle way, then, is being assertive—our third approach. Being *assertive* means standing up for our rights, stating what we want or need with self-confidence, while keeping in mind the rights of others. Passive and aggressive responses are the actions of immaturity. Assertiveness is the adult approach. Mature people are able to assert what they want and need, while gaining or keeping the respect of the people around them.

### Direct Instruction

Assertiveness is a skill that not only can help the individual but also can benefit a whole classroom or school. Assertiveness reduces bullying, tattling, and fighting while creating an atmosphere of mutual respect. In teaching students assertiveness, you might begin with a minilecture defining assertiveness and contrasting it with passiveness and aggressiveness. Give students the following example:

Sixth grader Gabe is standing behind Marianna waiting to leave the classroom. He keeps playfully poking her in the back, just to get a reaction. Here are three different responses:

- *Passive*: Marianna ignores Gabe, hoping he will stop on his own.
  - The result: Gabe keeps poking harder until it really hurts. Marianna starts crying, and Gabe gets in trouble with the teacher. Marianna may begin to develop a victim mentality, and Gabe may become increasingly angry and resentful.
- *Aggressive*: Marianna turns around and digs her sharp fingernails deep into Gabe's arm, yelling, "Stop it, you jerk!"
  - The result: Both Marianna and Gabe get in trouble with the teacher, and both vow to "get" the other person as soon as they get a chance. Ongoing classroom disruption occurs.
- *Assertive*: Marianna turns around and says clearly but quietly, "Gabe, please stop poking me right now. If you keep it up, I will have to tell Mrs. Jacobs."
  - The result: Gabe stops, saying, "Geez, you don't have to be so touchy." No one gets in trouble, and Gabe is less likely to poke Marianna again.

Create a poster with some sentence starters students can use when they need to be assertive. Here are some ideas:

- I understand that you _____, but I would prefer _____.
- When you _____, I feel _____.
- You are ____ (doing/saying something), and I would like (prefer) _____.

- Please stop _____.
- Excuse me, but _____.
- I appreciate it when you _____.
- I don't like it when you _____.

Give specific examples of how students might use each one:

- I understand that you are angry at me, but I would prefer it if you didn't yell and swear.
- When you hum while I'm trying to read, I feel frustrated.
- You are sitting too close to me, and I would prefer it if you moved to a table that has more room.
- Please stop tapping your pencil.
- Excuse me, but I don't like being called Samantha; call me Sam.
- I appreciate it when you read silently to yourself. Thanks.
- I don't like it when you text while you are driving.

### Role-Playing

For guided practice, place a poster with the sentence starters from the previous activity somewhere where students can see it, or give students cards with the sentence starters listed on them. Ask for some volunteers to act out a few of the situations listed here, first passively, then aggressively, then assertively, using one of the sentence starters you've given them. In each case, you play the person who is being annoying. The audience/class may be invited to help out, if necessary. After each of the responses, discuss what the consequences or results of that response might be.

- During a test, a student (you) keeps trying to copy answers from the volunteer.
- You are standing too close to your partner and telling her about something that happened on the bus.
- You are calling your partner a goody two-shoes for doing so well on a math test.
- You are asking your partner to give you his or her lunch money.

- You are telling your partner every detail about a movie he or she plans on watching.
- You keep poking your partner playfully.
- You keep calling your partner by his last name or by a nickname you make up.
- You use a loud voice when talking to your partner.

### Independent Practice

Invite students to come up with realistic situations at school or home that might call for an assertive response. Have them write their scenarios on index cards. Collect and screen the cards. Then you might use the Inside-Outside Circle or Musical Circles to provide a structure for role-play practice. Once students are paired up with partners, have Partner A do what it says on his or her slip of paper and have Partner B respond using one of the assertiveness sentence starters. Then switch roles, trade cards, and repeat as needed. You might want to circulate among the students and coach them as needed.

## Teaching Strategies: Interrupting Appropriately

### Class Meeting: Interrupting

Open the meeting by asking students these questions:

*Defining Questions*

- What does it mean to interrupt?
- What kind of interruptions are there?

*Personalizing Questions*

- Have you ever been interrupted? How did you feel about the interruption? The person or people who interrupted?
- Have you ever interrupted others? What happened?
- Do you know people who interrupt a lot? Discuss.

*Challenging Questions*

- What are the consequences of interrupting inappropriately?
- What are the benefits of interrupting appropriately?

### Direct Instruction

Teach the following three steps, using a poster, the overhead, whiteboard, or other visual aid.

1. If you *must* interrupt a person's conversation or phone call, stand where you can be seen.
2. Wait for that person to acknowledge you or signal for you to come back later. (Unless it is an emergency—discuss what constitutes an emergency.)
3. When it is time for you to speak, begin with "Excuse me for interrupting, but. . . ."

Remind students also to be specific and to the point with their request of information, and to thank the person for his or her time.

### Practicing Interrupting Appropriately: Yada, Yada, Yada

STEPS

1. Pair students up.
2. Direct one partner in the pair to simply repeat something like "Yada, yada, yada" until the partner signals that she wants to interrupt.
3. The other partner follows the steps for interrupting appropriately and makes a simple request or gives some information. (You might give some suggestions.)
4. Switch roles.
5. Practice until each student has achieved mastery.
6. Have one or two students demonstrate.

## Teaching Strategies: Disagreeing Respectfully

Disagreements often turn into arguments or fights because one or more of the people disagreeing doesn't know how to disagree respectfully. He or she may say, "That's stupid" or "That sucks!" which often quickly progresses to "*You* are stupid!" or "*You* suck!" You can imagine where it goes next.

### Direct Instruction

Teach students the following steps for disagreeing respectfully:

1. Listen to the other person's point of view using your empathetic listening skills. Use a neutral facial expression and body language (no eye rolling, head shaking, etc.). Don't interrupt.

2. Summarize his or her point accurately, without any value judgments.

3. Say, "I disagree with your idea (or opinion) because _____." Fill in the blank with concrete supporting details (examples, facts, logic, etc.).

### Practice Disagreeing Respectfully: Line-up Activity

This activity is taken from Kagan (1994). Explain to students that you are going to give them statements of opinion. If they strongly agree with the statement, they are to stand shoulder to shoulder (with some elbow room between them) facing you toward one end of a designated line. If they strongly disagree with the statement, they are to stand at the other end of the line. Others are to place themselves on the line in a spot that represents how strongly they agree or disagree with the statement. Some suggestions:

- Capital punishment should be imposed on convicted murderers.
- Country (or rap or emo—you know your audience) is my favorite music.
- The best pizza in town is at _____.

Any statement that will generate a variety of opinions is good. You probably know what your students feel strongly about.

Once the students have lined up according to their opinion, make sure they are in one single line facing you. Count off half of the students, and ask the half that is to your right to take a giant step forward and turn around 180 degrees, facing the opposite direction. Next have them slide down to their left until they are opposite someone from the other line. Have them stand close enough to their "partner" to hold a conversation. Tell them that they are going to practice disagreeing respectfully. Designate one line A and the other B. When you say "Go," students in Line A are to express their opinion on the topic, including concrete supporting details for their opinion. After about 1 minute (maybe less—your judgment call), stop them, and ask Line B to disagree respectfully using the three-step process you just taught them. Sometimes people in the middle of the line don't have a strong opinion either way. Ask them to try to take the opposing position just for the sake of practicing the skill of respectfully disagreeing.

Afterward, hold a class discussion on the activity: What did students notice? How does it feel when someone disagrees this way as opposed to the way students often disagree? What things are worth trying to change someone's opinion on, and which are not? Which way of disagreeing has a better chance of changing someone else's opinion?

## Teaching Strategies: Accepting "No" and Other Nonnegotiable Decisions of Authorities

The purpose of this particular social skill is to help keep students from making matters worse when they don't get their way by whining, nagging, throwing temper tantrums, and violently lashing out. Gandhi, Martin Luther King Jr., Susan B. Anthony, Nelson Mandela, Rosa Parks, and many others accomplished what they did not through emotion alone but through the combination of reason, passion (and compassion), *and* action: the Head, the Heart, and the Hand.

### Class Meeting: Accepting Decisions of Authorities

*Defining Questions*

- As kids (or teenagers), a lot of decisions in your lives are made for you. Who are some of the *authorities* in your life who make decisions for you? (Try to keep them brainstorming instead of going off on a tangent here. Refocus by repeating the question.) What kinds of decisions might they make that affect you?

*Personalizing Questions*

- What are some examples of times you disagreed with a decision made by an authority but accepted it? What happened?
- Are there times when you did not accept the decisions of authorities? What happened as a result?

- Are there times in your future when you may have to accept decisions of authorities? What might the consequences be if you choose not to accept them?

## Challenging Questions

- What are the difficulties or costs involved in accepting decisions of authorities?
- What are the benefits?
- Do you think the benefits outweigh the costs?
- (The following questions are geared more toward high school students.) Were there times in history when certain people believed that the costs did not outweigh the benefits of accepting authority and did something to challenge the decisions? Who and when? *How* did they go about creating change? What did they sacrifice? What can we learn from them?

You might follow up this class meeting by emphasizing that education's role is not to create sheeplike citizens who blindly follow authority no matter what, but rather to learn when and how to challenge authority, and what issues are worth challenging and what issues are not.

### Direct Instruction

Teach the following steps in accepting no and other decisions of authorities:

1. Look at the person and listen carefully.
2. Breathe, check your body's "hot spots" for tension, and relax on your out breath (4 seconds).
3. Using a calm voice, say, "OK" or "I understand."
4. If you disagree, discuss it later when you've calmed down. (Use the disagreeing respectfully social skill.)
5. Avoid whining, arguing, pouting, or throwing a tantrum.

### Practice

First, talk about the decisions of authorities you have to accept if you want to keep your job. For example, I might tell students there are some rules I find unnecessary, but it's part of my job to enforce them. Or, I may not want to perform bus duty, but that is the extra duty I was assigned, so I do it. Then, you might model this skill for the class by pretending to take an important phone call. Pretend the call is from the principal, telling you there will be an emergency faculty meeting after school, or from your spouse, asking you to skip something you enjoy doing and come home immediately after school. Here's an example:

"Oh, excuse me class; I have to take this call. It's really important. . . . Oh, hi, Holly! . . . You have a doctor's appointment? Are you OK? So, you want me to skip my run this afternoon and come right home to take care of the kids? (Breathe, relax) OK. Hope you feel better. Talk to you later."

Next, have students write down on index cards some decisions of authorities that they face or will face. Here are some examples:

- You can't have that expensive birthday party you wanted because your parents tell you finances are tight.
- You can't stay over at your friend's house on Saturday night because your mom needs your help.
- You have detention after school for arriving late to school three days last week.
- Your coach announces you won't be starting the game on Friday.

Next, using the Musical Circles, Inside-Outside Circle, or another pairing activity, have students practice the procedure for accepting decisions of authorities. Make sure that after each pairing the students trade index cards and repeat.

## Curriculum Connections

There are ways of connecting the content of this chapter to almost every content area.

### English Language Arts

- Ask students to develop some of the stories they told during the empathetic listening Musical Circles activity into final drafts of first-person nonfiction narratives.

- Ask students to engage in perspective taking in literature (similar to the activity described in Chapter 5) and try to empathize with different characters in novels or short stories.
- Students might do the same kind of research assignment as the social studies suggestion listed later, using famous poets, authors, or playwrights as their subjects.

### Languages Other Than English

Ask students to research and share cultural differences in manners, proximity, body language, and social skills.

### History or Social Studies

- Assign students to research portraits or photographs of important historical figures or present-day world leaders and analyze their feelings based on their facial expressions and body language. Then research when that portrait was done or photo was shot, try to discover what was happening in that person's life at that time, and compare/contrast what their initial impression was with what the person may have been feeling based on what they learned was occurring in his or her life.
- Students might research and report on people who challenged decisions of authorities, why they did so, how they did it, and what they accomplished.

### Science

- Assign students to research and report on the biochemistry of emotions.
- Assign students the same kind of research project as the social studies suggestion, using famous scientists as the subjects.

### Visual and Performing Arts

Students might do the same kind of assignment as the social studies suggestion, using famous artists, musicians, dancers, actors, and other performers as their subjects.

- Students might be challenged to express pure emotion through painting, movement, vocal expression, or music.

### Health/Physical Education

- Assign students to research and report on the connection between positive relationships and physical wellness.
- Assign them to research the impact of anger, stress, feelings of isolation, and other emotions on physical or mental wellness.
- Students might study the social skills and manners involved in good sportsmanship.

## Conclusion

This chapter does not provide every social skill that all students will need in their lives. That would most likely take not a book but a series of books. This chapter does, however, provide students with some of life's most important general skills: using basic manners, identifying emotions in themselves and others, being aware of nonverbal communication, empathizing, and listening. It also provides students with specific social skills that all students will need, from shaking hands to accepting reasonable decisions from authorities. These skills will help them not only in the classroom but throughout their lives as they experience that which brings the most joy, satisfaction, and meaning in life: positive relationships, relationships, relationships!

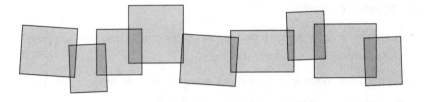

# 9 | CREATING AND SUSTAINING THE INSPIRATION

So far in my career, in my own classroom and as a consultant, I've worked with thousands of students. I have personally used almost every activity in this book. In all my years teaching these ideas and skills, only about a dozen students have been completely resistant to SEL. And these were students whom I had only a day or less to work with. With more time to build a relationship, I believe I could have been successful with these students, too. Most kids learn this stuff enthusiastically. Some complain, and you'll hear terms like *touchy-feely* tossed around, but even those students become engaged when you start using the interactive strategies. Students will participate and learn well if five criteria are met:

- The relationship between the teacher and the students is positive and trusting.
- The relationships among the students are generally friendly and supportive.
- Students understand how participating in SEL and character development will benefit them in both the short and long term.
- You really believe that it will make a difference in students' lives.
- You model the skills yourself.

As you begin to engage your students in SEL, assess the level of trust between you and the students as well as among the students. If the students seem to be resistant, take some time to do some team-building activities; have some open-ended, student interest–centered class meetings; and play some noncompetitive games with them. Bond through cooperative play. It doesn't take long to build a positive relationship with and among students if you show them you care enough about them to get to know them and have fun with them. Developing trust also requires that students perceive you as competent to teach what you are teaching, and to see you as "with it," organized, dependable, and, ultimately, in charge. Covey (1989) calls this combination *character and competence.*

As you take the time to build trust and develop positive student-teacher relationships, students are simultaneously learning about and interacting with each other in positive ways. They get to know each other differently than they would just sitting in class and working together. Also, once they begin the initial SEL, you will find that these activities serve to maintain and strengthen the bonds you've established. Put students from different cliques in cooperative groups in fun, engaging activities and stand back and watch the walls between them crack, then crumble, and then come down entirely. The original group of students I referred to previously as the Choice Players was an amazingly diverse group of about 15 kids: ages from 9 to 18, boys, girls, rural, urban, suburban, black, white, Latino, gay, straight, poor, middle class, athletes, a former gang member, a camouflage wearer, a couple cheerleaders, and a spiky, tattooed superpunk. After two full days of team building and SEL training, and even more so after our first big presentation, these kids became a tight-knit unit. They may have looked, dressed, and spoken differently from each other, but under the skin, they were just great kids enjoying learning and spending time together.

Finally, modeling SEL is critical to its success. Students, especially adolescents, can detect hypocrisy a mile away. For example, if you are teaching students to take responsibility for their behavior and then make excuses for your mistakes or blame them on someone or something else, the disconnect will be obvious, and your students will resist. In *Zen and the Art of Public School Teaching,* one of the author's main messages is that students may not learn any of the content of your class, but one thing they are always learning is who you are (Perricone, 2005). They are always watching you, even when you don't know it, and what you model is what they learn. As Albert Schweitzer said, "Setting an example is *not* the main means of influencing others. It is the only means!"

## Sustaining the Initiative

Imagine that you have a successful experience teaching the skills and concepts presented here, which is highly likely if you attend to the criteria just described. To ensure success and to sustain the initiative of *Inspiring the Best in Students*, you and your school need to address four other criteria:

- *Professional development*: sufficient training for teachers to implement the program.
- *Focus*: sufficient time devoted exclusively to social and emotional (character) skills.
- *Models and mentors*: opportunities for students to observe and work with positive role models and adult or peer mentors.
- *Parent and community involvement*: a coordinated approach among the school, parents, and community organizations to SEL and character development.

### Professional Development

As I have stated, I truly believe that you can read this book, implement the strategies as they are explained or modified as necessary for your students, and have an integrated and successful SEL/character program in your classroom or school. If you are an individual teacher, this could be a lonely proposition. If it is a schoolwide effort, having a faculty book study may be a cost-efficient approach. But (1) to convince the resistant faculty that this kind of instruction is worthwhile and not just "this year's new thing" or "this year's bandwagon," (2) to inspire the "middle-of-the-road" faculty members, and (3) to affirm and sustain the energy of the "cheerleader" teachers, high-quality, engaging staff development can't be beat!

At the end of this section, I'll list some resources for staff development. Although there are many others available, I can only vouch for those listed. Be wary of programs that tend to be packets of glitzy posters, reward systems, and sayings. Look for programs that offer

- intensive (multiple-day) initial training that provides a research-based rationale and uses best-practice pedagogy;

- ongoing support throughout the year(s), including additional training, preferably including a practicum or some kind of mentoring program (this is the guided practice component of a good professional development program); and

- observation and feedback on implementation.

It is equally important that school leaders attend the professional development sessions along with the faculty and staff. The school's or district's success in implementing a school- or districtwide initiative depends to a large extent on the leaders. It is their responsibility to provide clear expectations as to the "big picture" of program implementation; support teachers and staff as they attempt to implement SEL; and create accountability for implementing the program with integrity, possibly including SEL or character development in the yearly performance review.

Another benefit of high-quality staff development is the positive impact it can have on adult relationships and the school culture. Going back to modeling, if students observe their teachers and other school staff interacting with respect, personal warmth, empathy, humor, responsibility, and fairness, it sends them a loud message. Some resources for staff development include the following:

- ASCD: www.ascd.org
- The Character Education Partnership: www.character.org
- The Collaborative for Academic, Social, and Emotional Learning (CASEL): www.casel.org
- The Center for Social Emotional Education (CSEE): www.csee.net
- Inspiration for Education (my consulting company): www.inspiringmotivation.com

## Focus

Sufficient time must be dedicated to SEL/character development for it to be effective. A one-shot blast of character at the beginning of the school year will be met with the same enthusiasm by students as "this year's new thing" might be by resistant faculty. And it won't stick.

Because SEL can be integrated into the curriculum or taught as its own subject, there are many ways "sufficient time" can be achieved. Some elementary teachers start every day with a class or morning meeting in which one aspect of SEL is taught or integrated. Many middle and high schools have an advisory period that might be dedicated to SEL. Or, if there is a team approach, maybe one or two teachers on the team teach the content, while others support it and integrate it into their curriculum. Maybe the English or social studies teachers would take it on, as almost every concept and skill can be integrated into those content areas. Another approach is one that a school I've worked with has used. Every Friday, a high school and elementary teacher team up and teach one social-emotional concept or skill to groups of middle and high school students. Finally, the school or district character education or SEL committee, with parameters set by the school or district leader, might simply take on the responsibility of designating sufficient time.

## Models and Mentors

In a school implementing SEL, everyone in the school, whether he or she knows it or not, is a model. Positive modeling of respect and caring by the leadership, regular reminders at staff meetings of the importance of modeling good social skills, and ongoing professional development regarding SEL can increase the degree and consistency of modeling's impact on students.

Schools generally have two kinds of mentoring programs: peer mentoring and adult mentoring. In some of the schools I've worked with, student leaders/ mentors are thoroughly trained in choice theory and SEL. The student leaders then act as table facilitators in schoolwide training with middle or high school students; conduct minilessons on SEL in elementary classes; frequently are assigned a younger student to be friends with at first, and later on to tutor or mentor; and also provide peer mediation. Some schools connect small groups of students to various members of the faculty and staff. In the Kensington Woods High School in Howell, Michigan, every adult in the school, from the principal to the school custodian, has a mentoring group, a small number of students they meet with regularly. The purpose of the meetings is first and foremost to build a connection. After that relationship is established, then quality mentoring can occur.

## Parent and Community Involvement

It seems there are two extremes regarding parent involvement. One extreme is the complete lack of it. At a typical school open house, maybe 20 percent of the parents attend. You send letters home requesting parent-teacher conferences and hear little or nothing back. At the other extreme are the "helicopter" parents who hover over the principal, counselors, and teachers, sometimes attempting to micromanage others' decisions and approaches. The latter is usually well meaning and can be pretty easily managed with tact and assertiveness. The former is, unfortunately, more frequent than the latter and offers more challenges.

Parents are not involved in their children's education for many reasons: they may not have time; school may bring back painful memories and feelings; the staff and faculty seem intimidating or unfriendly; they may not speak English well or at all; and so forth. The following considerations may increase parent participation:

- How regularly and frequently do the district, the school, and teachers communicate with parents? And how do they communicate? Not every parent has a computer, but some use the computer exclusively for communication.

- Where do you ask parents to meet? If at the school, is the school door open when they arrive, or are they met with a locked door and no clear explanation of how to gain entry?

Once they get in, are they met by a human or a sign? When they report to the main office to sign in, does someone greet them with a smile and a "Welcome!" or a look suggesting that they are just another irritating interruption? Would it be possible to meet at another location or at their home?

- What is the parent-educator ratio at meetings? Do parents feel ganged up on? Would it be possible to have someone meet and greet the parents at the door and then walk them to their car after the meeting, and ask them how they are feeling or if they have any other questions?

- In parent conferences, meetings, and presentations, do you use "educationese" or language that parents can understand?

- How do you communicate to parents that we respect and care about their child?
- How can we make parents' involvement needs satisfying?

  *Survival*

  - What can we do to make sure they feel emotionally safe?
  - Do we provide clear expectations of what we want from them?
  - Can we provide food and beverages?

  *Love and Belonging*

  - How do we create a sense of "we" instead of "us and them"?
  - How do we communicate that we value and respect their involvement?

  *Power*

  - How can we make their involvement meaningful to them?
  - How can we help them see the school as a place for their own personal growth and parenting education?
  - How can we provide parents with a voice in their children's education?

  *Freedom*

  - How do we communicate to parents that there are as many ways of getting involved as there are parents?
  - How can we help them see that the time they give is time well spent?

  *Fun*

  - How can we make involving themselves in the school community enjoyable?

Community involvement is the final important characteristic of high-quality character education or SEL. One of the best ways I know to connect the school and community is through a highly effective teaching approach that aligns perfectly with and enhances SEL, character development, and intrinsic motivation: *service learning*. Service learning is "a teaching method where guided or classroom learning is deepened through service to others in a process that provides structured time for reflection on the service experience and demonstration of the skills and knowledge acquired" (Berger-Kaye, 2003, p. 7).

Service learning teaches academic curriculum through service to a community. The community may be another classroom, as when older students read to younger students or tutor them in literacy. Or it could involve students working in an animal shelter, growing food for a local food pantry, or visiting and reading to people in elder care facilities.

The critical difference between what many schools require, community service, and true service learning is the curriculum connection. SEL is not an add-on. And there are dozens of organizations just waiting to partner with schools in many different ways. *The Complete Guide to Service Learning* (Berger-Kaye, 2003) is a wonderful resource for educators interested in connecting their students with community agencies and organizations. Service learning is also an excellent way for students to practice the social-emotional skills they've learned in a real-world setting.

## Conclusion

Before you set the book down, I'd like you to consider some of the tragedies we have experienced as a human community in the last 50 years: September 11, 2001; school shootings from Columbine to Virginia Tech; the violence in Tiananmen Square; genocide in Uganda; ethnic cleansing in Serbia; mass suicide in Jonestown, Guyana; the untimely death of dozens of promising young musicians and actors, including Jimi Hendrix, Kurt Cobain, John Belushi, and Heath Ledger. All of these sad events are due to a lack of social-emotional skills or the presence of serious character flaws. These are the infamous examples. We all know stories of personal tragedies, and there are millions of others that we either don't hear about or can't keep track of because of their sheer numbers.

Social-emotional skills and character development are essential for our students in their pursuit of happy, successful lives and satisfying relationships both in and outside school and later in life. If more people are achieving these goals, the community, society, and the world are all the better for it. SEL and character development, then, are not just important; they are crucial to the future of our children, their children, and the world. If having this knowledge and these skills can have such a profound impact, they must be taught intentionally. Finally, it is the attitude of the individual educator that can make the most profound difference between a successful SEL or character initiative and a failed one. Whether you truly believe that you can inspire the best in students or not, you are right—so believe that you can!

> The way is long—let us go together.
> The way is difficult—let us help each other.
> The way is joyful—let us share it.
> The way is ours alone—let us go in love.
> The way grows before us—let us begin.
> —Zen invocation

For each row of word clusters, assign a 5, 4, 3, 2, or 1 next to each word group. A 5 represents the word group that is *most important* to you; 4 would be next, 3 next, 2 next, and 1 would be *least important* to you. You must use all five numbers in each row. When you are finished, use the scoring key on page 72 to determine your internal profile.

|  | C1 | C2 | C3 | C4 | C5 |
|---|---|---|---|---|---|
| **R1** | ___ family<br>friends<br>cooperation | ___ achievement<br>goals<br>purpose | ___ choices<br>self-reliance<br>free will | ___ play<br>pleasure<br>enjoyment | ___ safety<br>comfort<br>shelter |
| **R2** | ___ independence<br>space<br>selecting | ___ neatness<br>order<br>procedures | ___ relationships<br>communication<br>closeness | ___ laughter<br>joy<br>amusement | ___ growth<br>strength<br>control |
| **R3** | ___ games<br>humor<br>fun | ___ health<br>caution<br>security | ___ novelty<br>change<br>freedom | ___ feelings<br>sympathy<br>helping | ___ learning<br>competition<br>high standards |
| **R4** | ___ pets<br>kindness<br>warmth | ___ spontaneity<br>excitement<br>celebration | ___ adventure<br>risk<br>outdoors | ___ recognition<br>being heard<br>winning | ___ dependability<br>punctuality<br>responsibility |
| **R5** | ___ challenge<br>skillfulness<br>work | ___ understanding<br>generosity<br>nurturing | ___ flexibility<br>travel<br>liberty | ___ stability<br>tradition<br>investment | ___ wit<br>innovation<br>variety |

Total Love & Belonging: _____     Total Fun: _____

Total Power: _____     Total Survival: _____

Total Freedom: _____

**MY INTERNAL PROFILE**

My highest basic human need: _____

2nd: _____

3rd: _____

4th: _____

Lowest: _____

# REFERENCES

Alderfer, C. (1972). *Existence, relatedness, and growth*. New York: Free Press.

*ASCD's learning compact redefined: A report of the commission on the whole child*. (2007). Alexandria, VA: ASCD.

Bennett, D. (2009, April 5). The other kind of smart. *Boston Globe*. Retrieved October 8, 2009, from www.boston.com/bostonglobe/ideas/articles/2009/04/05 /the_other_kind_of_smart

Berger-Kaye, C. (2003). *The complete guide to service learning: Proven, practical ways to engage students in civic responsibility, academic curriculum, and social action*. Minneapolis: Free Spirit Publications.

Berkowitz, M. W., & Bier, M. C. (2005). *What works in character education: A research-driven guide for educators*. Washington, DC: Character Education Partnership.

Blum, D. (2002). *Love at Goon Park: Harry Harlow and the science of affection*. New York: Berkley Books.

Boffey, B. (1993). *Reinventing yourself: A control theory approach to becoming the person you want to be*. Chapel Hill, NC: New View Publications.

Cohen, J. (1999). *Educating minds and hearts: Social emotional learning and the passage into adolescence*. New York: Teachers College Press.

Covey, S. R. (1989). *The seven habits of highly effective people*. New York: Simon & Schuster.

Erwin, J. (2004). *The classroom of choice: Giving students what they need and getting what you want*. Alexandria, VA: ASCD.

Frankl, V. E. (1984). *Man's search for meaning.* New York: Simon & Schuster.

Frost, R. (1975). *The poetry of Robert Frost* (E. C. Lathem, Ed.). New York: Holt, Rinehart and Winston.

Gardner, J. (1985). *Grendel.* New York: Vintage Books.

Glasser, W. (1975). *Reality therapy.* Los Angeles: Colophon Books.

Glasser, W. (1986). *How the brain works* diagram. Los Angeles: William Glasser Institute.

Glasser, W. (1998) *Choice theory: A new psychology of personal freedom.* New York: HarperCollins.

Glasser, W. (2000). *Counseling with choice theory.* New York: HarperCollins.

Goleman, D. (1995). *Emotional intelligence: Why it can matter more than IQ.* New York: Bantam Books.

Goleman, D. (2006). *Social intelligence: The revolutionary new science of human relationships.* New York: Bantam Books.

Gossen, D. (1992). *Restitution: Restructuring school discipline.* Chapel Hill, NC: New View Publications.

Hawes, A. (1996). The evolution of animal play. *ZooGoer, 25*(1). Retrieved on June 1, 2009, from http://nationalzoo.si.edu/Publications/ZooGoer/1996/1/junglegymes.cfm

James, W. (1892/1962). *Psychology: Briefer course.* New York: Collier. (Original work published 1892.)

Jensen, E. (2006). *Enriching the brain: How to maximize every learner's potential.* San Francisco: Jossey-Bass.

Kagan, S. (1994). *Cooperative learning.* San Clemente, CA: Kagan.

Klem, A. M., & Connell, J. P. (2004). Relationships matter: Linking teacher support to student engagement and achievement. *Journal of School Health, 74*(7), 262–273.

Lickona T., & Davidson, M. (2005). *Smart & good high schools: Integrating excellence and ethics for success in school, work, and beyond.* Cortland, NY, and Washington, DC: Center for the 4th and 5th Rs and Character Education Partnership.

Marzano, R., Pickering, D., & Pollock, J. (2001). *Classroom instruction that works.* Alexandria, VA: ASCD.

Maslow, A. (1943). A theory of human motivation. *Psychological Review, 50*, 370–396. Retrieved October 12, 2009, from http://psychclassics.yorku.ca/Maslow/motivation .htm

*Merriam-Webster's collegiate dictionary* (10th ed). (1996). Springfield, MA: Merriam-Webster Inc.

Ornish, D. (1999). *Love and survival: The scientific basis for the healing power of intimacy.* New York: Harper.

Payton, J., Weissberg, R. P., Durlak, J. A., Dymnicki, A. B., Taylor, R. D., Schellinger, K. B., & Pachan, M. (2008). *The positive impact of social and emotional learning for kindergarten to eighth-grade students: Findings from three scientific studies.* Chicago: Collaborative for Academic, Social, and Emotional Learning (CASEL). Retrieved from www.casel.org

Perricone, J. (2005). *Zen and the art of public school teaching.* Frederick, MD: PublishAmerica.

Ryan, R., & Deci, E. (2002). *Handbook of self-determination research.* Rochester, NY: University of Rochester Press.

Scieszka, J., & Smith, L. (1996). *The true story of the three little pigs.* New York: Puffin Books.

Snodgrass, M. E. (2008). *Beating the odds: A teen guide to 75 superstars who overcame adversity.* Santa Barbara, CA: Greenwood.

Thompson, M., Grace, C., & Cohen, L. (2001). *Best friends, worst enemies: Understanding the social lives of children.* New York: Ballantine Books.

Toppo, G. (2006, June 20). Big-city schools struggle with graduation rates. *USA Today.* Retrieved June 24, 2009, from www.usatoday.com/news.education/2006-06-20 -dropout-rates_x.htm

Wubbolding, R. (1991). *Understanding reality therapy.* New York: HarperCollins.

Wubbolding, R. (2000). *Reality therapy for the 21st century.* Philadelphia: Brunner-Routledge.

# INDEX

Note: Information presented in figures is denoted by *f.*

# ABOUT THE AUTHOR

In his 11 years as a middle and high school English teacher, **Jonathan C. Erwin** has also coached track and cross country and directed plays and musicals. From 1996 until 2003, he was a staff development and curriculum specialist with the Board of Cooperative Educational Services (BOCES) in upstate New York. Jon has been an adjunct faculty member of Elmira College and a part-time professor at Lock Haven University, and is currently a senior faculty member of The William Glasser Institute. He recently completed his work as director of training and curriculum for Smart Character Choices, a three-year character education initiative based in Michigan.

As an independent educational consultant, Jon has spoken and presented his highly energetic and interactive workshops throughout North America as well as in Europe, South America, and Australia. He lives in western New York State with his wife Holly and three children, Nate, Liam, and Laena. For information on training or consulting, visit his Web site at http://www.inspiringmotivation.com. Jon can be reached by e-mail at jon@inspiringmotivation.com and by phone at 716-433-3949.

## Related ASCD Resources: Inspiring the Best in Students

At the time of publication, the following ASCD resources were available; for the most up-to-date information about ASCD resources, go to www.ascd.org. ASCD stock numbers are noted in parentheses.

**Books**

*Activating the Desire to Learn,* by Bob Sullo (#107009S25)

*Activating and Engaging Habits of Mind,* by Arthur L. Costa and Bena Kallick (#100033S25)

*The Big Picture: Education Is Everyone's Business,* by Dennis Littky and Samantha Grabelle (#104438S25)

*The Classroom of Choice: Giving Students What They Need and Getting What You Want,* by Jonathan C. Erwin (#104020S25)

**Multimedia**

*Emotional Intelligence Professional Inquiry Kit,* by Pam Robbins and Jane Scott (#997146S25)

*Project-Based Learning with Multimedia* (CD-ROM), by the San Mateo County Office of Education (#502117S25)

**Video**

*High Schools at Work: Creating Student-Centered Learning Three Tape Series with Facilitator's Guide* (#406117S25)

*Educating Everybody's Children, Tape 4: Increasing Interest, Motivation, and Engagement* (#400225S25)

The Whole Child Initiative helps schools and communities create learning environments that allow students to be healthy, safe, engaged, supported, and challenged. To learn more about other books and resources that relate to the whole child, visit www.wholechildeducation.org.

For more information, visit us on the World Wide Web (http://www.ascd.org), send an e-mail message to member@ascd.org, call the ASCD Service Center (1-800-933-ASCD or 703-578-9600, then press 2), send a fax to 703-575-5400, or write to Information Services, ASCD, 1703 N. Beauregard St., Alexandria, VA 22311-1714 USA.